'This story is dedicated to all the Staff and Customers that ever worked or visited my Bistro'

INTRODUCTION- by © Rosalind Hopewell.

Hello, let me introduce myself to you. My name is Rosalind Hopewell and this book is a light hearted view of running a bistro. It's told not only through my words and experiences, but also through the imaginary words and views of an improbable insect, Frankie the Bistro Fly. He is the voice of what I believe goes on when I am not around, and what he sees that I don't. He also has the joy of being my shadow. Remember as you read my experiences he is always there to enhance them, well from his view anyway!

I've written this for the sheer fun of it, though it took a lot longer than I anticipated… but what doesn't. That's the fun of life I guess, is the anticipation, and that was a major factor in the buying and then running the Bistro. Because no matter what I planned, expected, it rarely worked out that way. So because it was a Bank Holiday I might anticipate it to be busy, no way, because Windsor Council are holding some event the other end of town. Come the following day I get a coach load of ladies who have been 'shopping in London' drop in for lunch, and totally throw us. But each day was different, and each one presented another challenge. Through the pages of this little book I have presented some of those situations to you and hopefully given some insight into the world of running a Bistro, but also some of the issues that really affect a business but most of all the silly, funny and stupid things that can make you laugh or cry.

I have written this tale in a diary type fashion, making it an easy read for whenever you have a few minutes to escape from your world. So share my experiences and I hope if you are thinking of changing your life and entering into a new project my words here will give you heart and perhaps a little bit of advice in preparation for your anticipated journey.

Most of all I hope you enjoy this tale as much as I did in writing it and living of it.

TABLE OF CONTENTS.

4

- **ROSALIND & FRANKIE - That's us the authors of this book.**

Frankie -Let me introduce myself I'm Frankie the Bistro fly.

I've been here about 4 years now, and I've had the pleasure of watching over the business since the day I moved in, well dropped in actually, and what a joy it has been, because no one knows I am here!!!

I first landed as a mere centimetre of a fly and I've grown quite nicely into rather a handsome chappie. I'm not your ordinary dirty fly, I'm a bit different to the rest, sort of a cross between a ladybird and a fly. Got some lovely red in my wings with lovely green eyes and I'm a sucker for cleanliness, no landing on the sort of shit that some the other guys do.

I didn't have much of a start in life, dropped at a great height by my parents onto the flat roof of the Bistro and left to fend for myself, I think because I was a bit of a misfit they (my parents) decided to dump and run. Anyway thankfully the window was open (leading to the toilets I must add, did not want to stay there), so I made my way down to the noise below and low and behold there was my future. All light and noise and delicious smells and so I found my spot and have overlooked the goings and comings of the place ever since. Oh and what a Royal story it is, I have landed in Royal Windsor...the home of the Queen... this is my story with some input from the owner - Rosalind.

Rosalind - That's me, the author of this Bistro Diary. Who am I and why did I decide to change my life in six weeks, well let me try to explain.

It is the year 2001 and I have spent around 16 years in the computer industry, working from a humble administration temp up to the glories of being a Director!! There is an interesting story to be told from those years, but this book is about the Bistro.

I was sitting in a Bar in Egham, skiving from work, as I was sick to death of the charade of a business I was working for. It was a nightmare, the job I was supposed to be doing just did not exist, and the management were so content on there big fat wages (and asses) everything was going nowhere!

I'd spent most of my life in the computer industry running around the world.

5

My previous job was customer relationship management Director, with the odd marketing, sales, consultancy and help desk involvement. Of course there was that monthly not to miss very important Board (bored) Meeting, which of course had to have the very important repetitive report produced each time. I did enjoy it for seven years, then our Chairman made the error of bringing in a new boy. One who could spend money, who thought marketing, was getting bigger budgets to spend on corporate entertainment. I'd had enough and resigned, he was pushed out not long after me. I spent 3 months having fun, him well who knows? I then spent the next 3 years in a variety of jobs, all within the industry, mainly specialising on the customer relationship side, basically how to use software to good effect, for both the company and the customer. Software similar to that used in the help desk/service centre of today, most companies still do not use it to any benefit for the customer....

So browsing through Daltons Weekly, (should you ever require finding a business, holiday home, franchise etc. this is the publication to research), enjoying a nice glass of red wine in one my favourite wine bars in Egham. Well there it is in black and white, Café for sale in Windsor, and the rest as they say is history, but not without an awful lot of pain, money, worry, learning, fun, laughter and finally satisfaction.

I bought half of the Café (as it was then), this seemed a good idea as it was my first one and the owner, Paul, seemed a reasonable guy. All agreed and monies changed hands on March 12th 2001 (it took six weeks to organise) I became the proud half owner of a Café in the centre of Royal Windsor.........and my eyes were opened to another world of business and incredible mayhem, well in this Café anyway.

On achieving the goal of owning your own business, a whole new world opens for you...you become the Personnel Officer, the Accountant, the Operations Director, the Managing Director, the Buyer, the Marketing Director, the Sales Person, the Health and Safety Officer, the Administrator, the DIY expert, and above all the 'GOFFER' and that one beats them all!.

Let me tell you if ever you are tempted to open a Restaurant, Café or any type of public eating/drinking place, you will need more energy than you have ever required in your life. You will need to be ready for every type of individual you can imagine walking through the door, you will have to smile and welcome them. Because these people, the general public are paying your wages, council tax, VAT, and everything to do with you making and having a living. These people are not always nice, and you do not know this when they enter the door.

My belief and to become my motto was 'You only fail if you let yourself fail.'

Everyone can find a reason for failure, there is always someone, or thing to blame, never yourself. Me, I was not going to fail, I may give in and re-route my path, a little like a traffic jam, same destination, just a different route, but I was not going to fail. I had made this change to my life, now I had to deal with it, my decision, my choice, and my game. Royal Borough of Windsor here I come!...........Wonder if I will meet the Queen?

- **MY TOP TEN TIPS FOR SURVIVAL** *(In no particular order).*

1. Everything you, your staff, your customers touch costs money.

2 Smile, customers pay the wage bill, tax, vat etc and are your lifeline to survival.

3. If you don't do every job yourself, even if just once, then you do not know the full cycle of your business.

4. Never rely on all the equipment working every day all day. Use your imagination for finding alternative ways of coping.

5. Staff are your all or nothing and can make the difference to success or failure. Hire them, fire them, but be there for them also.

6. Remember it's a business first, a lifestyle second.

7. Good days are much shorter (in length not numbers) than the bad ones, so enjoy them to the full.

8. Keep some money in reserve at the start, you will need it for the most unexpected things and hidden costs.

9. Learn from your mistakes, and don't be afraid to try the idea again, when you've worked out how to make it work.

10. If it all fails, at least you had the guts to TRY

BE YOURSELF AND BELIEVE IN YOURSELF AT ALL TIMES.

- **MY FIRST TENDER STEPS INTO BISTRO OWNERSHIP -
ooh, aah, ouch!**

Frankie - Do I feel drained, Rosalind has been working seven days a week non-stop for 10 hours, and I have been flying around after her. If she can learn the business this quickly, guess I had better make the effort too. Must admit getting a bit wearing on the old wings, she never sits down and goes from one end of the Bistro to the other in nano seconds. Dives downstairs every minute for some supply or other, flies off to the cash and carry for bundles of goods every other day and on top of this has a 13-mile drive home to Windlesham every night. No wonder she's taken to stopping at the local pub for dinner!

Her biggest problem is the guy, (who owns the other half) he struts around the place like lord muck. The best one was a Saturday lunchtime, I must admit I'm pretty laid back chappie, but this took the biscuit. Paul strolls into the Bistro, which is packed and Rosalind is running around all over the place. He only stands by the till shouts to Katrina to make him a coffee and get him a Danish..........Rosalind's response was somewhat rude, she still forgets that customers have ears!! The Royal Borough of Windsor attracts a vast array of tourists from all around the world, luckily not all understand the English profanities. I do believe I am going to have to read a little dictionary over the next few weeks to understand them myself!

Rosalind - One of my first ventures into the catering arena was at the tender age of 17 at a Pontins Holiday camp in Brixham, Devon. I also did a stint at the Norfolk Hotel in Bournemouth as a chambermaid, got promoted to Housekeeper. Followed by a season helping out a friend of a friend in her Café and Guesthouse also in Bournemouth and finally a year on the Isle of Wight working day and night as either a barmaid, waitress, and chambermaid, sometimes all three in one day! This was my working experience until around the age of 21, with a few other little jobs thrown in, i.e. Window dresser, Estate Agents receptionist (where I taught myself to type) and the glory of being an assistant in a jeans boutique along the way. Then I got on the travel bug, and finally before entering the world of serious employment became a partner in a record shop back in Bournemouth, with the odd night of DJ'ing as well. Then at the age of 28 years entered the IT world for 15 years!!

So with this in-depth experience, 20 plus years later I am back into catering. Now after weeks, months, years, I have lost track of 10 hour plus days of learning all over again how to be a waitress my energy is low.

The Bistro, well café as it was when I bought it, is a going concern so basically from day one the doors were open and we were serving the general public. I inherited some staff, which proved interesting, their general opinion was to sit back and watch me as I attempted to get a handle on the business. Hence my involvement with the previous owner, whom I thought may be of assistance.

Not the case a typical example is as follows:

'Paul (still half owner) was beyond a joke he comes in like the ultimate pratt and orders coffee and Danish pastry from Katrina, our hardest working member of staff. She manages the giant coffee, frothy milk making machine, but also the dishwasher, the cold drinks, the odd pastry and occasionally lending a hand to the Chef! This demanded in the middle of Saturday lunchtime. I somewhat rudely point out that most of us had been here since 7:30am and not had time for a glass of water let alone eat. He still ate the bloody cake whilst leaning against the till, how I did not push it down his throat I don't know...it was the last Saturday Paul stepped into the Bistro. His previous faux pas had been to arrive with his whole family and sit down for lunch, on a Saturday and then expect to get it free...where we could have had paying lunch customers.'

Over the coming weeks I became everyone's shoulder to heave worries and concerns on. It seems all the staff had some grievance or another and as the new owner it seems I was the one to take them all on. The manager, Alfredo, turned out to be the biggest crook out, one way of getting more money is to do extra hours, when there is something to do! It turned out that Alfredo would come in at 7am on a Saturday to get ready for the rush, apparently to fill up salt and pepper pots, wrap cutlery, prepare tables etc. So when I turned up at around 7:30 am I expected to see the salt pots full, cutlery gleaming (I know it's only a Bistro, but it is in a Royal Borough!). Needless to say they were not. Note taken. Next was his notorious attitude to being a Manager, which would be him taking precedence over anything any of the waiters/waitresses required. i.e. ordering from Katrina drinks, if a cappuccino was sitting there for one of the other waiters order, Alfredo would pick it up to fulfil his order rather than order another one. Hence the waiters order was delayed, causing some confusion and argument, most annoyingly affecting the delay of our

10

service to the customer. I was somewhat incensed by this. Note taken. Several points came out, during the few weeks that I allowed Alfredo to continue being Manager, many notes were taken. Finally the last note complete, I got rid of him!

I tend to be the sort of individual who gives people enough rope to hang themselves and watch. What everyone underestimated about me is that above, and beyond anything I was going to make this run down café a successful business, and where chaos reigned I was going to put in logic and order. Alfredo went, and with him a certainty that we would loose some customers, the ones who seemed to not understand the menu prices…the Alfredo specials as we called them. More certainly we would gain a new type of customer, the ones that paid the menu prices and would appreciate the new regime.

If anybody has the opinion you just open the door and the rest is just 'play' for the owner of an eating establishment, let me remind you of some of the sheer frustration felt and energy required in one day.

On average I guess I must walk 5 miles a day, this is just backwards and forward from tables to kitchen to till etc. What is more annoying is the extra ½ mile added for the "I forgot to order this, or can I have a glass of water". Having been used to the best part of my day in my past life spent in traffic, (yep M25), and desk sitting, flying, conference, meeting etc. sitting…my feet are feeling a little sore.

After six weeks I could barely put one foot in front of the other, and each night I used to sit and wonder what the hell I had done. The suppliers all confused me with their quotes and deals, which one way looked good but with minimum purchases, say of 3 boxes proved to be wasteful. It seemed Alfredo had deals with them all, if he bought 2 got one free etc. trouble was most of the deals were around things like trays of cakes, mostly getting thrown away after 3 days, so all waste and no profit. My guess was Alfredo was selling them on! How the hell Paul left him in charge, God knows, he obviously did not do any stock checks or balancing of the books. Well all part of my learning curve.

I felt, for the first time in my working life absolutely helpless and with no one to turn to for help or advice.

My first sign of beating the supplier was gaining a penny off the price of a sausage, trust me that equalled £££££'s of savings during one year, and no one cared. All my friends thought it was great I had escaped the world of IT, but not one of them had a clue about running a Bistro, and the price of sausages is not something everyone wants as a dinner conversation!
.

After seven weeks I was crying myself to sleep and could not bear the thought of the alarm going off at 6:30 am. And I still hadn't started opening evenings, we opened at 7:30am and closed at 6pm. I had never felt so alone and so unable to cope, my energy level was down to zero, my social life had all but disappeared and sex, what is that!!!

3 months had passed, when I finally thought I could take no more and would collapse, I think I was very close to total cave in. To save the day and me, my lover (a complicated affair) decided we would take a long weekend in Geneva. Now this was going to be a test as it would be the first time I would leave the Bistro in someone else's hands. The business had now become almost like a child, and I was very protective of it and would loathe leaving it with someone else, even though that person was Zuzana and about the best you could get

So with my last ounce of resource I organised everything, ensuring no hiccups could occur (well as best I could). Stocked up, (Saturdays being our busiest day), enough change to keep a bank, lists made out for the ordering, wine and beer bought (still doing cash and carry at this stage for these items) it was like preparing for war. Dealing with the public is quite often exactly like going to war, and being prepared is the better option, so I left with trepidation, but at least I felt I'd left them with full ammunition!! I escaped and had a glorious long weekend away, thanks to my lover and thank you Geneva!!!!

- **OH KNOW, ITS EXAMS - I wasn't brilliant at school, what now?**

Frankie - Got a feeling today could be fun, Rosalind is off to take exams and she's only been here weeks! The staff are still not that sure about her and so there's bound to be a bit of gossip going on today. First off they don't all arrive on time, Zuzana is meant to be opening, which is okay as she's the most experienced, but she does have to have a cigarette and coffee before she's anywhere near worth talking to, and she's an addict to the crossword in the Daily Mail, which sometimes takes over from the customer!

Zuzana is here on time, but not with the usual half hour, so instead of opening, i.e. chairs, tables etc outside, she's entranced into crossword, cigarette and coffee, Rosalind would not be happy. Katrina is the next to arrive, albeit 15 minutes late. She is the queen of the coffee machine and the hardest worker out of them all. Now there is a bit of an atmosphere of late between her and Zuzana, Rosalind is not aware of this as she only sees the sunny side of them all. Anyway today it seems things are not all that well between the two of them, Katrina has already ignored two orders from Zuzana and its only 9:30 am. Guess I'm going to have my work cut out today to watch and listen.

To summarise there is a minor fight in the kitchen, basically Atilla our chef is in one of his 'off moods' and being generally awkward. Zuzana and Katrina are still at each other until mid-afternoon. The others all seem to be acting normal, as in doing what they should be doing although not too enthusiastically. I don't think Rosalind would be too pleased.

Rosalind - After weeks of 10 hour days, your own business does not give you the grace of late mornings, I am still learning, the Café was now a Bistro opening from 7:30am until around 6pm I am ready to take the exams. First is the Licencee exam, an 8-hour day of constant questions and reading with a 50 plus question exam at the end of it. I should explain that I had worked a 12-hour day before this challenge and was completely exhausted mentally and physically.

Apparently I must get my name on the licence to continue to sell liquor, so this is a priority.

It should be noted that I am still learning one end of the coffee machine from the other. How to take an order from a customer whilst checking in a delivery, and maintaining harmony between the staff...all at once. So a licence exam should be a breeze, me thinks not.

It's a hot day and I have the teacher from hell, having read the licensee book already, admittedly between serving the customers, I am not overjoyed at going through every paragraph again. This darling teacher did not once let me be, every question he asked I was the target for an answer. I can not remember how many times I was asked how many times you open and close on Christmas Day, and what age people can drink and what they can order, and in what situation. For instance a 16 year old can order Beer, Port, Cider or Wine if they are eating. All this after two weeks of physical abuse to my feet and body, via the Bistro and not to mention the 12 hour beating up the day before, I was tired.

The importance of the exam is highlighted in that the first 16 questions cannot be answered wrong, if any are you instantly fail and therefore do not get the licensee certificate, you can re-sit it. Knowing my lack of patience and attention to detail (with administration) I do not think I could take it again. I passed and I must say it was down to the teacher and his nagging that got me through.

I can now bore everyone with the licensing laws of this country along with the hygiene and health regulations. That was another fun day, this time surrounded by motherly volunteers working for the local community.

- **DELIVERIES AND SUPPLIES - Its not all smiles and easy shopping!**

Frankie- I'm having a bit of a day off today, some family members dropped by last night and we had a great shindig. Journeyed up the road to a rather large bar in the Royal Windsor central station. Well we had a riot, met a load of flies and bugs from all over Windsor, rocking away to the music, nicely hidden from the public below. Got rather tipsy on the spillage from the more boisterous revellers, only takes a couple of sips and we are a little flightless! Took an age to get home, kept getting lost, the others didn't really know the way and I was rather leaning on their wings for support.

Hmm I also met a rather feisty little lady fly that lives locally, but I cannot for the life of me remember where! Hopefully I told her where I abide.

Having slept late, and risen at lunchtime in time to watch the latest scenario of the day. Oh dear another delivery, it's the 3rd today so I've overheard, and this one unwisely has chosen the lunchtime…oops.

Rosalind - You would think that all suppliers to eating abodes would understand there is a particular pattern, that being breakfast, lunch and dinner being, hopefully the busy periods. So why is that around 1pm you will get the biggest delivery of the week arrive with the driver standing around waving his delivery note for someone to sign, today this seems to be allocated to me. He stands waiting for me to check the order and in this case try to find space where he can dump the stuff. I ask you please 'dump' yep that's what they do and run! Just in case you call them back for the odd box of chips they've forgotten to deliver, or is it they forget or just need to make up someone other establishments order, me being the cynical type.

Meanwhile the whole place is bustling with the 1-hour lunch brigade, in other words they have no time to spare. The staff are irritable and somewhat unhelpful in the area of taking a delivery, there has already been two and I was not around..oops. So it's down to me to remove the hassle from the back door. Now I have always taken my fair share of the work in the Bistro and deliveries fall into that category. We actually get quite good guys doing our deliveries, but not today it's the 'holiday fill in temp', bugger. This therefore means he is a jobs worth, looks at me with disdain as he hauls all manner of boxes and

15

cartons of drinks into the back passage and dumps them. This is also our fire exit by the time the guy has left I am standing at the end of the hall hemmed in by boxes, unable to pass back into the Bistro. Hence I end up walking out of the fire exit do a hike round to the front of the Bistro to walk in to the staff glaring at me and asking where have I been ? 'There's a delivery, and we are one member of staff down on the floor, we needed you!' exclaims Zuzana. I carefully point to the back exit, which is stacked with boxes, 'buried behind that', I bemoan and smile.

One of my little hates is the supplier phone call, now this is a subject close to my heart. They know the business we are in but always ring at lunchtime! They believe they know who you are and your type of business, and it is always a male, sorry guys but that is the way it is, you always phone at the wrong time! You point out to them the time of day, but they continue with their onslaught of sales spiel, absolutely unaware that I am telling them I am not interested, or ring back later. I must admit I have put the phone down in many a mid-conversation, often only to be rung back and told we were cut off!!! Guess these guys have their common sense terminated before being allowed to use the phone, because they certainly don't use it!

CASH & CARRY.

Frankie - Thought I'd venture out with Rosalind today. She's off to Cash & Carry and talks about it as if it's the journey to Hell. It just can't be as bad as she bemoans to anyone that will listen to her, so it's up to me to judge this event.

I'm sitting in the back of her little jeep, she really needs to do a bit of a spring clean in here, obviously been on the golf course again, the shoes are covered in mud! Rosalind really ought to keep up her appearances. I bet the Queen doesn't have mud on her golf shoes, well if she plays golf. Have met some real Royal household bugs, may have to find out that little bit of information out from one of my pals who live up the hill in the Castle.

Well here we are, rather looks like an old warehouse, not that I know what they look like only got an idea from a mate of mine who lives in one. Must take up his invite to visit, would make a lovely overnight stay. I'm flying ahead of her as need to have a good look at this place from Hell. Well it's certainly got high ceilings, loads of space for a fly to dive around in. Great

16

shelves to snoop along and for some reason not a fly in sight? Here Rosalind comes, oops that trolley looks a bit out of control, she really ought to try pushing it folks!

After about 10 minutes I am getting very, very cold, it's all freezers and air conditioning, now I know why there are no flies in here, need to get out of here fast..............guess my mate must be in a somewhat more less food orientated environment.

Rosalind - So I thought I could drive a trolley!!

The ultimate shopping trolley from hell is located at Cash & Carry near Slough. It's 3 times the length of a supermarket trolley- with no sides or brakes!! You can only pull it, its wheels have no co-ordination and taking corners is an incredible achievement if done by the fourth go....

The pleasure of Cash & Carry is un-measurable, its dirty, mind bogglingly stocked in the most un-coordinated way. It takes the muscle of a body builder to lift and stock the trolley, let alone haul it along aisle after aisle hunting for the right stock, which is never where it makes sense to be. And it is bloody freezing, all cold counters, fridges and no heating whatsoever.

You queue longer to pay than you have taken to stock the whole trolley, which is now 2ft plus high with everything from beer to toilet rolls. People with a 'certain attitude' usually man the checkouts. They unload the trolley you have just lovingly stacked and balanced whilst counting and scanning, then re- load it all onto another trolley with no thought of goods being balanced for me to pull away. This leads to another queue for the goods to be counted, hopefully matching the number on the invoice, usually counted several times as numerous items are hidden underneath quantities of beer and toilet rolls. This of course creates another queue, and low and behold there is only one person taking the money. IF the gods are against me the dark gentleman in front of me is paying a £1,000 plus bill in cash, most of it in small denominations. But if I am really lucky I get a trainee cashier thrown in too, mercy!

Now I only have to unload it all again at the Bistro and if I am really lucky I will still have staff willing to help! I do love the Cash & Carry experience, not!

- **THE STAFF - They are there for you, but you had better be more than there for them**

STAFF VOCABULARY.

Frankie - I have a lot of fun watching Rosalind work with her foreign staff, not only is their English hilarious it also stems into sign language. To let them understand the difference between a fridge and a freezer Rosalind has a particular door opening movement for fridge, these are all upright, and another movement for freezers, these are all chest so open from the top. In fact she's got the sign language off to a tee, her impression of cutlery items is very amusing and explaining the difference between a fork and a spoon was a challenge, she kept forgetting a fork has four prongs, not two, at least I think she forgot?

Rosalind - Now working with Northern Europeans from the reaches of Hungary, Poland etc. there is quite often a language difference. There is also a great use of sign language on my behalf, for instance a fridge is now a 'pull and open' arm movement, a freezer (these are chest versions) is a 'pull up' arm movement.

Days off have become 'off days', bank account became a 'bonk' account (and no they did not understand the implication!). The word baked, as for baked beans became 'bak-ed', as did toasted and any other word with ed on the end. It became worse when one of the girls became hooked on crosswords, god did I need to know my English, finally I took in the biggest dictionary/thesaurus I could find, this actually proved to increase the nightmare, as they started looking up words and asked me to explain the explanation!

This collection of European tongues occasionally causes a fluster amongst the more elderly of my customers. One very fastidious older lady was privileged to hear the conversation that one girl had an 'off day, need to bonk, but on no account would anyone bonk with her!' The private comment to me that 'she was such a pretty girl and what would her mother think' left me very confused, when she explained exactly what was said I laughed. Poor dear was very shocked and had the impression that I was running a brothel and restaurant combined, I carefully explained I didn't have the energy to do both!!!

STAFF EXPRESSIONS

Attila our Hungarian Chef (we've had a few chefs in our time but Attila, no puns please, lasted the longest) came out with one of the best comments. We have an open kitchen, and we all were guilty of shouting from some distance to the Chef, usually to be heard above the customer noise. Our favourite and most often call is 'Mayonnaise' (always that extra calorie laden sauce required to add to our delicacies) and Attila obliges with a pot. So Attila, after a particularly busy session looking quite straight faced at me and states "I've changed my name to Mayonnaise as that's all I get called", and smiles. He definitely got the English dry sense of humour.

STAFF LETTER.

There is only one occasion where I really thought I needed to put in writing a subtle warning to all staff, the following is a copy of that letter:-

Dear All,

As you are aware it is now a couple of years since I bought the Bistro. I have been lucky enough to find and keep hardworking and loyal staff throughout most of this period.

I believe everyone has been fairly paid and well treated. We have quiet times and we have hectic and mad busy times, but all of you are given constant work and regular hours in either scenario.

I have left you all to be honest not only with me, but, with yourselves. I don't question what you eat or drink, I believe you know there are rules, some written and some not, and I hope you abide by them.

The reason for this letter to you all is that over the past few weeks I am receiving more and more comments from staff and customers. These concern actions of some of you, the way your are dealing with some customers and the interactiveness between you all as a team.

It is imperative as we move into the winter months that everyone concerned with working in the Bistro takes a pride in it, and realises that the 'customers' pay our wages.

I would also remind everyone that everything that is sold or bought through the Bistro is also seen by both the tax and VAT organisations that monitor my input to them. In doing so they also monitor what profit should be seen each month from what is bought and sold. I remind all of you of this, as now we are over a year old it would be expected that my accounts would be inspected. This does not concern you, but brings great pressure on me to ensure everything is being run honestly and smoothly. So I ask all of you, and please this is not aimed at anyone specifically, just a reminder to everyone. Please if you are going to give a discount, have a drink or 'forget' to ring in a table, think twice about what you are doing to the Bistro and me.

We have had a lot of fun and heartaches together, I want to work towards us all having a real fun Christmas and an end of summer party to relax with. And hopefully there will also be enough in the kitty to include a bonus for each of you.

Here is to profit, happiness and success.

Regards, Rosalind.

PC STOLEN

Frankie - I've come for a day out today, I'm down in the basement and visiting Rosalind's' office, bit of a mess down here, but no cobwebs thank goodness. It's quite large and there's lots of interesting bit's and pieces to swoop in and out of. The staff change down here as well, god some of their shoes could do with a day in the fresh air...I'm just taking my afternoon siesta when I'm disturbed by footsteps, so I fly back into Rosalind's office to keep out the way. Well you could swat me with a wet lettuce leaf, in comes Sebastian with a very large holdall, what's he doing in her office? I'm sitting very still on the top shelf, don't want to be seen, he's always struck me as a bit of a fly basher. By gum he's taking her laptop, what can I do? I shoot past him and up the stairs and make as much noise as possible, but every machine in the place is buzzing, grinding and hissing.... I fly right past her ear, 'go down stairs now' I shout, but she doesn't hear. Oops here he comes, there he goes smiling goodbye, its his last day and he's off with her laptop...oh no she's writing her book on that, and she uses it to talk to people, well she talks to it a lot so I guess there must be someone listening?

Rosalind - I am a fairly trusting individual and I have never had any real trouble with my staff, except one, that being Sebbie, steam coming out of my head here as I write!

Still in my learning curve at the Bistro, (well it never really stopped!) I was not a great one on stock checks, as I did most of the ordering I went on my instincts to some degree and also the logic of checking deliveries. I am not one for great detail, though eventually in my role as restaurateur I became much more aware of the smaller items requiring my attention, and the need to do so.

Anyway I digress, during the months that Sebbie was with me, I always sensed I was out on things, like I could swear there were 2 packs of bacon in the freezer, and then there was one. But because it was more subconscious than actual I never gave it a second thought, mistake and another learning curve.

On Sebbies' last day he brought in a big bag. The changing room is downstairs next to the storeroom with the freezers. On leaving, having paid him in nice new bank notes. His country, Poland does not accept old ones. On leaving the Bistro I note he looks somewhat fervently back, and his bag seems heavier. I go downstairs look into freezers, but no all is okay, I have got a little more alert in the last couple of months. Into my office, something is missing but, what? Suddenly it dawns on me my laptop is no longer sitting on my desk. I rush upstairs shouting to my staff, luckily no customers around. The guys go running out to find the culprit. No joy. It's not the laptop, its crap and broken and only works when you hold the wires together.

It's what is on it that I need? All my e-mail addresses from long ago, all sorts of documents and information I have collected. I bemoan all this to one of the girls who asks if I am going to call the police. I tell her yes otherwise I cannot claim the insurance. She asks me to give her 24 hours. I have no contact for Sebastian except the mobile, which funnily enough is switched off. He is on his way home next day, and no one seems to know where he lives here in England, shit.

Next day I am the owner of my old laptop, and Sebbie has gone home with some serious bruising to explain to the family.

As most of the people working from me are foreign students they have an honour amongst them, they do not put each other in jeopardy by stealing or lying to their employers. One word on the street and whoever the rogue is will be found, and he was much to my delight, I just wish they'd taken his money as well, would have paid for that bacon!!

A STAFF NIGHT OUT

Well now and again I thought they deserved it! So it's off to Royal Windsor Races, 15 of us, including the gay Sunday piano-playing singer, who always adds that extra 'fun' experience. As he spends much of the time sussing out who is the most camp among the patrons of the Bistro, this done whilst he is singing! There is guaranteed to be a few watching the horses.

Windsor is a lovely racecourse and still seems unspoilt. All the modernisation that has gone into some of the other courses around the country has taken away the 'human/horse' atmosphere. With Windsor you can sit outside, champagne glass in hand, under a sunshade, and actually see the horses strolling past to and fro from their paddocks. Get the ambience of the place and feel the grass (if you take your shoes off), smell the odours, yep real horse shit, and you are only yards away from the real action of the racecourse when it all takes off. Oh, best of all you catch a boat from the riverbank of the Thames in Windsor that takes you to the course. This is nicely situated outside a rather posh and pleasant wine bar called 'Browns', very entertaining in itself on race nights. All aboard, and there you are a nice little bar on board so time for a quick drink to start off the evening.

If you have been lucky, the jazz band is playing after the last race with the wine still flowing, and you can manage to entice yourself away you can catch the last boat back to town....otherwise it's a taxi, which can prove a very long wait. It seems quite a few people miss the last boat.

So I have organised my merry gang and we have the tickets for the boat, yep did a little 'tasting of the vino' at Browns. Took over the back seats of the boat, why do youngsters always want back seats! Race tickets I have pre-purchased, you do get a bit of a discount. That's a bonus, still 15 of us! First race at 6:15pm and we are offffffffffffffffffffffffffffffff

With race cards bought, wine ordered and tables arranged, all outside and umbrellas at hand as clouds are looming, the aim is to place the first bet. Now none of my guys have been racing before and of course I'm considered a pro. as I've been many times, so can I give some advice? Their understanding of the situation is that as I've been here before I must know the horses, it takes me a bit of time to explain that the horses are different at each meeting. Their thought process is at each meeting each week the same horses are running, so I must know the best one by now! I explain my only professional experience is I go by the colour of the silks and perhaps the name of the horse when I bet. This does not help with the choice of bet, so we now have a mixture of Polish, Slovak and Hungarian, (two of us are English) going into an in-depth discussion of which horse and how best to choose it.

I can honestly say that after 'much ado about nothing' colours were chosen, horses selected, yes we did view the beauties as they strolled in their finery. Bets were placed and we actually saw a race in the flesh. The other attraction is there are huge screens to view the races scattered around the course, and one was just above our table, enabling us to enjoy the wine, food & laughter.

STAFF

Frankie- Well, so to say 'as a fly on the wall' there are a few things I could tell Rosalind about her staff, somehow I have a sneaky suspicion she knows most of what I could tell anyway! She has this rule that they are not to smoke at the bar in the Bistro when customers are eating nearby. Now it may be that those tables closest to the bar are the smoking ones, but rules are there to be broken, so it seems. As soon as she's out of the place they light up, and also whilst at it break her other rule of not all speaking in any language other than English! Mind you I think sometimes that them not conversing in our mother tongue is a good idea, I get the impression they discuss some pretty hot stuff sometimes. I must get some of my fellow comrades over, those that have learnt the lingo from their time spent watching and listening in their establishments. I've got one in a Butchers, a couple in the Browns Bar overlooking the River Thames, (bit posh for me), and a few fellows scattered around the various eating abodes of Windsor. Of course they are not all so lucky as to have three nationalities to listen to. Well that's not including English or any of the many foreign tourists that visit the Bistro chattering away in some unrecognisable tongue.

Rosalind -The thing with staff is they can be the make or break of a restaurant. Most of my staff are students from countries like Poland, Hungary, Czech Republic etc., which means they are on rotas of varying hours each week. They also take holidays with very little warning, because they get cheap deals for flights at the drop of a hat, or their friends are driving back home so they can cadge a lift. This means that I can sometimes get rather stitched up with the results of these capers. Below is a list of those that were significant on and off through my time with The Bistro, and overall were loyal and trustworthy.

Zoltan- the heartthrob.

This young man stole a bit of my heart the moment we met. He immediately put out his hand to shake mine when introduced and from that moment he always held a special place in my heart. Zoltan came from Prague and was the favourite waiter with all the customers, his charm and wit let alone the good looks ensured we had our fair share of lady customers!

I am pleased to say he is now travelling the world working on cruise ships as a

Food & Beverage Manager and we still keep in touch.

Zuzana- serious but sensitive, and is as honest as the day is long.

This lady from Slovakia was a very hard person to get to know. We had quite a few run ins, she left me twice! Somehow though we managed to find an even footing and worked as a very successful team, and became my manager, therefore was my right hand in the business. I trusted her implicitly and god knows you have to have someone beside you that you can rely on. We became and still are good friends.

Zuzana is now working very successfully in a travel office.

Susie- wore her heart on her sleeve and lets everyone know, good or bad!

Now here we have a young girl who is desperate to be loved. Which meant quite a selection of boyfriends came and went during the couple of years she worked for me. Trouble was she was in love within weeks and looking for marriage and babies! Hence the ever changing names of her fellas. My only problem really with our Susie was if she was not having a good relationship day, and we had a customer not having a good day it could prove interesting…a waitress from heaven or hell! She is now happily married.

Kirsti- very girlie, tall blond and blue eyed.

Kirsti came as a Saturday girl, she turned into an excellent assistant in the kitchen, which seemed to be where she preferred. Saturdays, being one of our more trying days, on the customer front, it suited her to be behind the counter!

She made it to Camp America to spend a season working with under-privileged children.

Katrina- the hardest working and the anchor of the drinks machine.

This lovely lady became the best cappuccino maker in the whole of Royal Windsor. People would come in especially to have her coffees, and she learnt the very special art of outlining a face or a smile on the froth with the chocolate.

Katrina came from Slovakia and her goal was to build a house and open a small restaurant specialising in local food. So far she has built the house! Gregory- Beckham look alike! Best saying 'it's not my fault'!

This floppy haired individual from The Czech Republic was a real charmer and thought that all women could not resist him. Thankfully they could so I didn't have another one with romance problems, well none that followed him to work. Our charming waiter, with a penchant for women, all of them!

Amine- moody from Morocco.

Our dark and moody man from the desert. He was a Chef with a little bit of an attitude, mainly towards the other staff. This all came to a serious upset one day, over presentation of a Panini! Next day all I found was a key posted through the letterbox and a note saying he wasn't coming back. Now that annoyed me!

Abigail- our Saturday teenager that became a little woman.

This charming schoolgirl came to us as a helper with the coffees etc. on Saturdays, she became Katrina's prodigy and learnt to make as good a cappuccino as her. Gradually Abi, as she was called became our Saturday angel, helping in all areas of the Bistro and the customers loved her as well.

She grew into a lovely young lady and I hope she meets all her dreams.

Eli- gentle and loved by all.

Another of my foreign ladies, Eli took over on one of Zuzana's sabbaticals and was an instant success with everyone...especially our Hungarian Chef! Now that would probably be a tale all by itself. Needless to say it proved a problem after a while, with them both gazing into each other's eyes and taking breaks together. After some gentle suggestion we got them working different shifts and slightly less involved when working together. She was the smiler that won over all our customers and charmed everyone.
Eli went home and made a successful career in office work.

Anita - our girl from Hungary.

The girl with the best broom technique in the county! Could our Anita sweep a floor! Another beauty from lands abroad, worked weekends and turned her hand at every job.

She now has a gorgeous little baby boy she has introduced to Windsor and training him to say Bistro!!

Attila - our Chef who makes the customers smile

Another individual who wore his heart on his sleeve. Having an open kitchen this could also be a problem, Attila was a smiling guy and always very helpful to the customers, we also did a very good take away service and he knew all the regulars. But if he had a bad day, then you could sense the mood as soon as you entered the Bistro and glanced his face. Luckily one of us could usually manage to make him smile, eventually.

Travelled to Spain, didn't quite like it there and now back working in Windsor.

Chris - our gay manager

Now here's a guy with loads of talent, but just doesn't really want to work. When we got quiet, he's the only one who would offer to go home! His sense of humour and way with the customers and staff out weighed his tendency towards being a sloth!

He and his boyfriend are still good friends and make wonderful party people. Chris is now making an album, his real true talent was singing and he has found a route to achieve this.

Sebbie – thief. Say no more.

Each and every one of my staff over the years has put some problem to me. It could be anything from boyfriend to where they are going to live, or have nowhere to live in one instance. This was Zoltan, so he ended up in my spare room for a while, that was a challenge.

My House Guest.

Zoltan, the charming young man from Prague. Due to a serious run in with the ex-manager of the Bistro, whom he rented a room from, he became homeless. Now me being a bit of a softy and unable to resist the eyes that smile, I let him come and lodge at my cottage for a few months!

Having spent months running the Bistro and going home to an empty house (well Vermouth, my dog was around then, but she didn't talk), it was nice to have someone to talk to who understood the nuances of my everyday life, and could talk 'Bistro Talk'.

So there was this handsome young man, it was like having your favourite meal on the table and not being able to touch it. Ladies you have all been there.......or wanted to. Anyway I digress. We built up a lovely relationship (platonic........ooh) and Zoltan even walked and looked after my beloved Vermouth when needed. I must admit over the months he was with me it did bring on the urge for male contact, physically that is. He left when his girlfriend came over, two of them I could not handle. But I must admit having Zoltans' company for those few months really helped me survive some of the most difficult times in my first year of managing the Bistro, so thank you to him xx

The trouble is the more you help and assist them the more they bring to your door, at some stage I thought I might have to hire a human resource person!! All their worries and fears, whilst in the background I was experiencing some of the worst personal problems I'd had for years...

- **CUSTOMERS - Love them or hate them- you need them.**

Frankie- I am not the sort of insect you will find in a toilet, I am much too particular for that. Though on some occasions I do visit the Bistro ones, more for keeping watch on things generally, we have a bit of a problem with the visitors to them. The Bistro is very long, narrow at the front and then widening out as you walk through, the toilets are at the back and upstairs, and you can't actually see them from the entrance. It seems though that the general public has discovered them.

Not a day goes by without some individual walking into the place and heading straight for the back, you can tell who they are by the way they storm through, or try to! Rosalind has got all the staff trained in halting these people, one of them is always on toilet duty...well looking at the door and ensuring they, the public are stopped in the middle of the path to them. You should hear the excuses people use to try to avail themselves of the facilities, if it wasn't such a pain it would be quite funny.

Examples are: - I'm pregnant (flat tummied teenager). I'm just meeting a friend, need to look around for her. (Place is empty). My child needs it, she/he is desperate, this being a ten year old, and 'oh I need to accompany him/her'. 'Oh I was here just now for a coffee and forgot to go'...need I say more?

A charity box was installed. So if the person is lucky, that is if we like them, they are polite, don't have six kids, or look as if they are on drugs etc., we let them use them, IF they put money in the charity box. Give Rosalind her due, it was her idea and she's made a fair whack for them, I think it's for the Oxfam shop over the road.

I was considering calling in the pigeons for the odd assistance whilst manning the toilets, but we all agreed that their feathers would probably get in the way, and more importantly damaged. Funny thing is most people seem afraid of pigeons, scum of the sky they call them. Me I think they are lovely chappies, give me loads of info on what's going down in Windsor...and I have found out they don't eat flies...now there is an endearing factor. Well anyway back to the toilets...if I must.

So my role in all of this is every now and again is to take a gander on what is going on upstairs, not that I can do a lot, but I can always call on a few mates.

Bluebottles (well not quite mates, they are not really my type) to come and bother the individual.... those bluebottles can really make a noise and they do fly rather well so can avoid the odd swipe with the toilet tissue. So we don't get the ladies sitting around to long, or you gents, you are just as bad.

Rosalind - Well where do you start, we have toilets at the back of the Bistro, which are upstairs, so you have to walk the length of the place to get to them. It's the bane of my life, every man and his/her dog seems to think we are a public convenience. From all walks of life, including the suited and booted, the tourist including the teenage kids, their parents and the odd lout.

One positive point is the charity shop across the road, we have a charity box that we suggest people make a donation to if they want to use the loo, and who are not customers. Over the past two years we have collected hundreds of pounds (it took me a year to think of the idea).

I wrote to the council suggesting they add to the signpost outside a significant pointer to the toilets opposite to me at the end of the street, some 1-minute walk from my Bistro. Here is a copy of that letter…

Dear Sir/Madam,

As the owner of the above named Bistro (it was on headed paper), I would like to bring a couple of issues to the council's attention.

1. *Could you please put a sign up pointing towards the local toilets under the car park in King William Street? I am totally fed up, as are my staff, with the general public walking straight through the Bistro to use the toilet facilities. They, the public get very rude when pointed in the right direction for the public toilets. As there is no sign I then get doubts and further conversation, taking me or my staff away from the paying customer. I look forward to your help with this very simple request.*
2. *As the Bistro is opposite the Bus Stop in Peascod Street I get a lot of trouble with the public that are queuing for the buses. I have tables and chairs outside (licence paid for), these are constantly used by these people. They throw cigarettes everywhere, use my ashtrays and move the chairs down the street so they are nearer the queue! They*

30

also block the entrance to the Bistro. Most are reasonable when asked to vacate the seats, but I do get abusive people, this is upsetting for my staff and does not give a good impression to any customers that do get a chance to use the outside tables!

3. One further matter, regarding the above and generally. I have noted that the street is not being cleaned. The pavement outside the Bistro every morning is full of trash from the nearby cash machine, cigarette ends and general debris. This now takes myself or staff five or so minutes to sweep the street before we can put out the tables and chairs. We are not open in the evenings so hence it is not down to my customers. We open at 7:30am, and I have seen your man out sweeping long before that time, so could he please do outside the Bistro also, thank you.

I hope you can empathise with the above points and help with the situation. I am aware there is a proposed plan to move the aforementioned bus stop. Hopefully the point I have made will be put forward. Generally the above concerns are having a negative effect on my business. I thank you for your time in reading this letter.

Yours faithfully,

Rosalind Hopewell

This ensued into a site visit from them to me, they had no idea the toilets were there, situated under the multi story car park in King William Street. It was delivered back to me it would be a great cost to put up the required sign, as they would need to replace the whole signpost. I would mention that in Royal Windsor the signposts are of a rather 'old fashioned design' guess to keep in touch with the overall image. Hence, the black iron posts that look as if they've been here for as long as the castle.

I wrote again to the council after a situation when I called the police after a rather drunken female demanded to use the toilets, which I refused. She wanted to see it in writing that it was only for customers, she threatened, she stamped she shouted abuse and generally was actually a bit frightening. So I called the police, which she seemed to enjoy, but funnily she disappeared when she heard they had answered my call and started asking for her description, seems this is a common occurrence when people are actually reported.

The other rather alarming occasion was a young lad who walked in, and managed to get straight past us all, we were busy. By the time I had spotted him he was nearly to the stairs. Well time went by and no sign of him coming down, this was a day of only girls being present, and so I sent one off to the luggage shop opposite the Bistro to get one of their guys to help us!

It took him about twenty minutes to get the guy out of the toilet, all I can say is I am sure drugs were involved somewhere as he looked rather 'out of it' on coming through the Bistro, and was none to polite either. The man from the luggage shop got a free coffee and the individual left with a large dose of 'flea in the ear'.

Oh the council still have not put up the signpost, and never responded to my second letter, guess they never will.

DRINKING REGULARS.

In My years in the Bistro it never ceased to amaze me how many people actually have a regular routine around a coffee/drink.

We had our Mr. Latte, at least 4 a day accompanied by the roll up cigarette.

Our Cappuccino and breakfast Panini couple, who always had the one Panini to share and one cappuccino with chocolate and one without!

The quick double espresso man.

The girls favourite the Eton Boys special, Mega Hot Chocolate with marshmallows and whipped cream!

The lady waiting for her bus 'cup of tea', which usually ended up in a take away cup as she never got the bus times right.

One of my favourites was the lady who always came in with The Times newspaper, she had a nice regular coffee and 3 biscuits. I used to stock biscuits just for her.

Another popular routine came when I introduced an offer of a glass of wine and hummus with pita bread at a great price after work, this brought in a lot of the ladies and gents in suits.

CUSTOMERS

Customers, that very important ingredient for the success of the Bistro. These are the people that pay everything. My wages, staff wages, my mortgage (no other income coming in), tax, rent, rates, every cost really that I incur in my business and private life, UGH. So it is with a smile every day from dawn till dusk that I greeted my guests, and it was not always a pleasant experience, but that's business!!!!!

Complaints...........Well okay we have had a few, but only one in writing, which went as follows:

(I have copied the letter verbatim, mistakes and all)

COMPLAINT ABOUT SERVICE IN YOUR RESTAURANT.

I'm writing to complain about the service I had in your restaurant on Wednesday the 26th of September around 1.30 pm. I spent the day with my friend in Windsor and after some shopping we chose your restaurant to have our lunch in. When the waitress brought our plates she spilled my class full of water and I got my trousers and jumper totally wet. She did apology (for several times) but I was very much surprised she didn't offer any compensation in the bill. At least I was expecting her to offer me a dessert or coffee on behalf of the restaurant, but there was nothing. You can only imagine how annoying it was to have my lunch with those wet clothes and it more or less spoilt the rest of our shopping, too. My trousers were almost dry when we left the restaurant but it wasn't until late in the evening when the jumper was dry.

I sure hope you would give some advice to your staff how to handle these kind of irritating situations. Obviously this waitress didn't know what to do and despite of her apology I have to say I wasn't satisfied at all. This is pity, because the food was good.

I did respond, and offered a drink, but never saw or heard from the lady again. One thing a customer forgets they can be as much the cause of the complaint as they can the telling of it. My waitress and Manager had a slightly different version to hers of this incident.

THE MOST DIFFICULT QUESTION

Frankie - I adore the busy days, I get a real buzz from flitting from wall to wall and listening in to the conversations and watching all the girls and guys tearing around. Good thing about busy days is no one is interested in me at all so I can be more adventurous with my coming and goings. I am now expanding my entourage of personal friends to other eateries within Windsor, and boy does that give me a lot of gossip to catch up with on my 'off days.'

Together we have invented a system to tell each other if there is a problem, this usually being a 'customer'. There is always a group of 'younger bugs' around that want to earn acceptance into the older group, so they are our messengers. Trouble is sometimes you get a Chinese whisper effect so the message can become a little confusing. For instance we had a customer in Bistro who complained about her breakfast, 'the eggs were runny', which transcribed to the bug messenger 'the customer's eggs are funny' which finally ended as a message to the tailors fly 'the customer's legs are funny'.

I have found out that customers bless them, are not just difficult here with us, well to Rosalind, they are down right difficult wherever they go. Can you believe a couple who came in to visit us, after eating double beef burgers, with the usual fries, followed by large ice cream desserts, stopped at Franco's (just down the road from us, a bit of a competitor, hey we need them) for large cappuccinos, and complained about the lack of chocolate sprinkled on top of the froth. I ask you.

Well I've organised a 'guess the most difficult question from the customer' evening. I think the humans call it a quiz night.

I've asked all my friends to watch and listen very closely to their customers over the next couple of weeks. We are going to take notes on all the questions they ask. Believe me do they ask some damn stupid questions. The best one I have heard so far is one of Rosalind's customers. They are leaving the Bistro, and look back at her and ask 'where exactly is the Castle? Calmly Rosalind

34

walks to the door and points up the hill, 'there', Windsor Castle being in full view, 'and before you ask I think the Queen is in!' she states.

Rosalind- I can guarantee that the most difficult, time consuming, annoying question in the everyday life of the Bistro is 'would you like ketchup'. For some unknown mysterious reason, no one, not one person can just say yes or no. Nope it is, um, don't know, do you (if it's a couple etc), brown or red. Now on a busy day with 20 customers to place orders and people wanting to pay, you just know you are going to walk back again to this table sauce in hand, and what is the next word out of the darling customer's mouth ' do you have mayonnaise'? Another mile added to my day, for that much needed item that will only add more calories to the light choice of baguette, fries and side order of garlic bread!

Of course we do have that daily, somewhat irritating question of 'where is the castle?' I should add that if you walk out of the Bistro and turn your head to the left, well Windsor Castle is at the top of the hill, may I add in full view. But does anyone look, nope no chance, they must all walk with their eyes down, perhaps they are looking for Royal Corgi dog pooh! Because you really cannot miss the bloody thing. But the never ending incoming coach, train, bus, plane, car, taxi, bike riding tourists do not look up!!!!!

I really think I missed an opportunity of opening a little table at the front of the Bistro..........'Information, Guide to Castle book and Souvenirs of Windsor provided here, free if you buy your lunch.............. well maybe.

ETON BOYS

Frankie- Urm. here they come again our little terrors, the Eton Boys. There is a famous school over the bridge from Windsor. Delightful flight it is to, all the way down to the river. I scoot over the heads of the swans, cross the Thames and fly down the old fashioned high street of Eton. Boy oh boy do these boys know how to dress, long coats with tails, and stripped trousers, just divine.

Anyway I'm off on a tangent...they love to visit the Bistro, Rosalind has built herself a little following I believe and she certainly knows how to handle these future 'lawyers, Prime Ministers, accountants, Wall street journalists, financial gurus etc.' If only their parents could see them after a few beers, and the odd bottle of wine!

35

There is usually a minimum of six and they wander down to the far table, this is surrounded by three walls, and has some very lovely murals on them, a bit like sitting in an outside cafe on the continent. I do tend to hang around this area myself sometimes, imagining the sun beating down on my wings, dreaming of lazily sipping a glass of the local vino, hearing a local guitarist in the distance, humming along, spying a glorious Senorita fly, speaking the lingo and dancing on the roofs...eer...back to Windsor.

Well six can sometimes turn into ten, and then they have the followers, I call them Eton groupies. THE GIRLS! They are the most up themselves people I have ever seen in the Bistro, smoking like there's no tomorrow and feet on chairs, their disconcert for the Bistro girls is unbelievable. If I were a bluebottle I'd annoy the hell out of them!

Rosalind - Oh good it's Saturday and 5pm, here comes the Eton boys. With respect to their parents, they really are a darn pain in the arse, well most, some have some rather nice ways with them, and the girls that follow them, well. Still I have a system and now they know if there are more than six I dispense of the rest, unless the Bistro is totally dead, then there are more rules. Like no bloody feet on the chairs, only two smoke at a time, god these kids with all that pocket money, credit cards and cheque books still blow it all up in smoke...almost a joke there!

The best time to see them was on a Sunday morning, all hung over and wanting the biggest breakfast I could supply. In they walk with their Sunday newspapers and unruly hair, trying very hard, I believe in some cases, not to throw up! There are a couple who stand out from the rest and are true gentlemen, respected the Bistro and the staff, and were always very 'almost flirtatious' with me. God help the girls when they become men.... or lucky girls, they were very charming young men. These guys are the element of what will be the 'upper crust' of our community, I hope they treat their advantage with respect.

36

CHILDREN FROM HELL

Frankie - There is a good point about children in the Bistro, they leave some very interesting mess behind them. As lots of mums bring in their children's food, you know the kind, 'can you heat this up in the microwave for 5 seconds type stuff', which actually drives all the girls mad. The concoction always comes out too hot or too cold, and leads to added hassle on a busy lunchtime.

Anyway if I am quick sometimes I can get to nibble on a crumb or two under the table before the girls get to sweep, I particularly like the dessert ones they bring in, stewed apple is very good. I also occasionally find the ultimate, like a complete hard boiled sweet, now those are good and I try really hard not to take a lick until I have washed them in the rain, or a puddle! No germs required, need to look after my health and maintain my post as the Bistro Fly, that's Frankie to you!

Rosalind-The Bistro is fairly children friendly, though the buggies are not that welcome, I believe some parents think their children have the god given right to do as they please, when they please, where they please. Some parents should be given serious advice on the expected manners of their 'little ones' in public, especially in a crowded Bistro on a Saturday!

The women push through the door with their earth shifting, crash proof buggies intent to get to the back of the Bistro. The best ones are the double seated terrain defying multi wheeled models driven by two women who are completely indifferent to the rest of the world as they push past numerous tables to get to the smoking section. There they can blow their smoke into the faces of the unknowing children and continue to ignore the world and gossip about the unfairness of life!

Many different people come into the Bistro and on the whole they are pleasant. But of course you always have the odd one. Our Saturdays are busy, they make a Sunday market look slow, we don't stop, every which way you turn there is something to be done, or someone to serve. I'm not complaining, just setting the scene.
So when you see a buggy with two kids entering the door about lunchtime, you sort of grimace a bit (well a lot actually), this particular buggy is being driven by a somewhat aggressive woman with a couple of others in tow. We do our best to keep our customers happy and make them welcome, but there

does have to be a bit of give and take, on a Saturday. Having seated themselves and dragged out several high chairs I turn my back to do other things. Children have a horrible piercing scream when they are trying to gain attention, well these two stopped the entire Bistro with that and banging of spoons on wooden trays. I froze, when I am angry I tend to go very cold and become very articulate.

Asking them respectively to consider other diners and keep the noise low I was greeted with are we children friendly. Yes, behaved ones that don't spoil other customer's enjoyment, "please leave" I request of her, with which she told the children to scream more as they were enjoying themselves, so she informed me. Encountering the removal of two screaming children, out of highchairs and a very mouthy woman in the middle of a busy restaurant is harrowing, especially as the woman continued to tell the children to scream whilst being wheeled out of the Bistro, meanwhile she is throwing abuse at me...I must admit as they left my customers applauded. I was somewhat drained, confrontation is not a pleasant experience, especially with a bunch of customers looking on......so I had a glass of wine!

- **TRAMPS, FLIES & SLUGS - All the additional ingredients that every Bistro requires to add that 'joie de vivre'.**

TRAMP.

Frankie - Well we have suffered a bit recently from a huge swarm of my cousins, aunts, uncles and long lost family, what a smell will pull in I ask you. Anyway me, Frankie being a clean sort of chappie I am not enamoured by the intrusion of these so-called relatives, or the damn smell. So I take a little trek to the great outside of my metropolis and view what is the cause of all this interest.

Well what a mess, honestly some of you humans should be put down at birth. I mean if I can be dumped at birth and find a home at least you lot, more intelligent species should be able to. There he is this lump of dirt making a home in an alleyway with no respect to anyone, and there are all my relations dancing around this scenario enjoying the situation. I ask you have they no decency, I know we are flies but there is a point we should not cross, well so I believe, hum............

It is human like, well not like I've ever seen before, rather more grey than the usual sort, and the smell, well rotting Pigeon pooh smells better, and I should know, they are my friends. There is a tatty moth ridden mattress, (hmm must learn more about moths) a broken chair, a menagerie of little insects and bugs amongst the boxes and rubbish scattered all over the place, God I hope none of them are related! It seems though that this is were the guy lives, and low and behold two friends turn up whilst he is out...

You couldn't make this is up if you tried, there is poor Rosalind at the back entrance, which happens to be the fire exit, looking at two of the dirtiest individuals you have ever seen. Their hair alone must hold a colony of my long distant relatives the 'flea'. They, the tramps, are absolutely out of their heads, swaying and singing holding cans and sitting on the stairs, with a carrier filled to the brim of. ......well I'm not quite sure...perhaps its housewarming presents for their friend...the odd duster etc...hee...hee.

They are completely chilled out and Rosalind looks as if she is going to explode, she actually speaks with some decorum. I must admit their response was good, never thought of having a summer and a winter home?

Rosalind - So I open the back door, which happens to be my fire exit and delivery entrance, and there sit two tramps with beers in hand, smoking and looking, well tramp like... you would think we would get a sort of decent type of tramp here, don't they know the Queen has her house up the hill.

"What are you doing here" I exclaim, after taking a somewhat needed deep breath. "Come to see our friend", they said smiling. Well I had spent months trying to get the tramp, assuming this was their friend moved on, and no one cared, except me, and of course my staff and customers! Now I had THREE. "Why is he here?" I asked, "it is summer" they replied in unison. Well sure clocks had changed, days were longer (still raining though), so technically summer I guess. "So" I responded rather incredulously. "Well, it's our mates' summer residence" they beamed at me through clouds of lager. At this point I had to smile and just asked them to make it a short visit.

These tramps also used to enjoy the odd fire in the winter. That is they used to start them and then walk off and leave them smoking in the maze of alleyways behind the Bistro. Within this area are the back entrances to probably another dozen or so shops, some of which are fitted with smoke detectors. It is not only on one occasion that I have opened the Bistro to find half the fire brigade lined up in the street, mostly looking somewhat bewildered as they empty shop after shop of personnel trying to work out which one is on fire! I did in fact several times inform them that it was the tramps setting things alight, usually I got a 'yes we know, but we need to check other avenues also'. Seems to me the tramps somehow always had the last laugh as their lives continued uninterrupted and ours were constantly being challenged!!

I'd called the council, the management of the block and not one person seemed interested. It's a bit difficult running a Bistro when you need the back door for deliveries etc. and a tramp is 'using the service area as a toilet', and general home base. Finally I stopped the police in the street and they actually helped. Well of a type, their first question was "which tramp is it", not being one for great detail I was not sure! "There are only two in Windsor, one's in the nick" was the answer. "Well I guess it must be the other one" I smiled.

Two days later all tramps had gone and the kind management of King Edward Court had actually cleaned the place...of a sort. They could have long ago got rid of him as he was breaking the vagrancy act, and it is private property. I just love management!!!

PIGEONS.

Frankie - I am prone to being rather nosey and in doing so learn quite a lot about our neighbourhood. Now I have become quite friendly with the Pigeons, they tend to leave my kind alone, I'm too much of an unknown for them to want to eat me. I have spread a vicious rumour that I am poisonous, and should I bleed will contaminate anything that touches me!!! I must admit the pigeons are also a good supply of gossip, as they are bigger than me...obvious to you...but they also fly higher and are just sort of accepted, even if loitering around Windsor High Street. Me I could get swatted if I get too near to the human race. So I always take time out to catch up on what is happening around town. So we have all come to an agreement that we will look out for each other, them to warn me of the fly eating monsters, the spider, me to warn them of the pigeon haters, humans!

Well the pigeons do seem to like landing on the Bistro roof, it's rather a suntrap and being flat once they've landed they just laze around and potter from one corner to the other. Problem is these birds do shit themselves a lot!!! I mean all the time, we are talking non-stop droppings, and boy oh boy do they mount up. Well Rosalind has to sort this out, as it is not a welcome sight, even though you can not sit on the roof, the customers can view it when passing to the toilets (very appropriate). A door opens onto it, which is great in the summer giving a cool breeze through the Bistro, but as for the view!

Here she comes, I must admit she does look rather funny with the rubber gloves and the various objects of dirt destruction she is carrying. What is even funnier is the short skirt and high heels, does she never carry spare gear with her to change into for these sorts of jobs, how long has she had the Bistro ....?!

Rosalind - Well more pigeon pooh encounter really.

It's been a long and intensely hot week, but today it looks like the rain is actually coming and last time this happened I walked into three inches of water running along the Bistro floor. Reason for this pigeon shit, there is a flat roof over the back of the Bistro and it is a party place for pigeons. I mean they send out signals to all pigeons flying over Windsor, that the Bistro roof is the PLACE to party, with ensuing result of mounds of pigeon pooh covering the drains. Thus ensuring with the first real downfall it clogs the pipes and we

41

have the overflows overloaded emptying down the walls of the Bistro, not pigeon pooh, just water I may add.

So with long stick, dustpan & brush, plastic bags and nose clip I climb onto the roof, I should mention there is a door opening onto it, so it's not all ladders and overalls. Now there is one hitch here, today I am in a short linen skirt, which when in bending position limits my movements, so pulled above my gleaming white knickers (may I add the big 'Bridget Jones' sort so modesty protected) I can bend and begin my work. With bum in the air and sweat pouring down my cleavage I manage to clear the shit away enabling me to see the drain openings, and rather proudly I have designed pigeon pooh protectors from plastic vegetable crates. I am chuffed.

This all being done, whilst running up and down the stairs to sort customers and take the odd order. It can be safely said I have washed my hands constantly and am making good use of the plastic bags as gloves, and of course pulled the skirt over the large white knickers.

Upon my last visit of the day for pigeon shit duty, I see two happy smiling faces from the flat overlooking the roof, guess they've viewed the white knickers. Well they are gay, won't do a thing for them, oops they are looking at the boob hence the smiles? But I also felt that maybe the pigeons where watching, funny they all seemed to be sitting on the walls surrounding the roof. I would bet on it they were going to have a party that night. I am glad to say it rained!!!

NOW THE FLIES.

Frankie - As I am a very far removed, distant relation of the fly, and I mean very distant! I must admit sometimes I think Rosalind is bit of a cruel individual, but on the other hand I understand her non-tolerant approach to my annoying cousins, very distant cousins.

It seems there's a bit of a gang trying to take over an area in the Bistro and causing a bit of a problem. I am a laid back sort of fellah, and enjoying a reasonable easy life here, so do not wish to have invaders causing me grief, and possible deadly consequences, even if they are related! There is a rather large group of bluebottles come to visit and believe they've found a new holiday home, well rumour has it. Spoke to a couple of pigeons who

42

confirmed this to me. Problem is I cannot have them around spoiling my lifestyle, they cause a hell of a noise and fly in all the places they shouldn't. Like right into the kitchen, and Rosalind is out to get them and that could cause me grief as well, depending on what tools of destruction she chooses to use. I am going to have to convince them to go. Rosalind is not winning so far and I think we could have a war coming soon if I don't persuade them to move on...

Rosalind – Where do all these flying creatures come from, I believe the flies are talking to the pigeons, because when the lights go out they are sending out party invitations to party, party, party. Not only on the roof of the Bistro but inside too!!

I have got fly spray (and used), insect repellent and those electronic zappers around the bistro, but those little buggers are always there when the lights go on in the morning. At first I thought the tramps had come back, you remember those little darlings from the back door, the most delightful fly attracting articles ever to walk this earth. But no, we have a new independent breed of fly, the bluebottle, the sort that watches you close the door at night and then comes out of the closet and 'flies'. I am convinced what they all do is watch with those little eyes of theirs during the day, from whatever crevice they can find setting themselves a flight pattern for the evening. This is of course after sending out numerous invites to local fellow flies.

Perhaps it goes like this, one Bluebottle to another:
Bluebottle 1 "See she's cashed up"
Bluebottle 2 "Look she's spraying the 'us' killer, again low level"
Bluebottle 1 "Look the lights are out, and that fluorescent blue light doesn't fool us"
Bluebottle 2 "No, we've seen our relatives lying in there"
Bluebottle 1 "Heard about last year and the sticky tape?"
Bluebottle 2 "No, but you are going to tell me"
Bluebottle 1 "Got so hot in here in the summer that all the glue melted, so we used it as a ski slope. Great practice for the hols!"
Bluebottle 2 "What you gonna do for the winter this year?"
Bluebottle 1 "Hibernate with pigeons on the roof and party, party, party!!!!"
Bluebottle 2 "Well think I might practise on that indoor ski slope!"

43

THERE'S A FLY IN MY PANINI!!

Frankie - It's a sad day today I've seen the death of close friend of mine, Bill from the butchers came over for a short visit. Wanted to view life from a more interesting aspect than just dead meat! So I invited him over for lunch and a general gossip. We chose to sit above table 10 as this gives a nice view over the Bistro and is not too far from the back entrance when its time to leave. Bill has been resident at the Butchers for, well forever, lovely chap and can tell stories like there going out of fashion. Always guaranteed a good chuckle with him, we also share knowledge of some of my staff as Rosalind uses his place for supplies, I'm always told if the chef has slipped in the odd chicken for himself! To be truthful though they always come back and tell Rosalind if they've put something on the bill.

Anyway Bill and I are in full gossip mode about the newcomer on the block, a real feisty lady who is living over in Cognito, the rather up market boutique across from the Bistro. Apparently she's got some right airs and graces about her, 'blimey she's only a fly' I tell Bill, but his retort is never heard, at that moment he gasps and falls straight onto table 10 into the guys Panini! I am totally gob smacked and just stare in amazement at the scene below...

Rosalind - Well when the customer called me over, I could see by his face there was a bit of a problem. Another customer complaint, the difference being a fly had fallen off the ceiling straight into the guys' lunch, dead I presume/hope, well we never got to check the heart. There was this large black fly, legs akimbo on its back in my customers Panini, well I said 'at least you know its fresh', after he had explained the incident. I must admit we both smiled and I gladly replaced the lunch.

My next bug story was another thing altogether. During the summer months we sell lots of salad, and despite the litres of water we use to wash the stuff there is always one little creature desperate to make its escape. On a particularly busy lunch session I am called over by a young lady sitting at our best and most observed table, by the double fronted window at the front of the Bistro. She is gently holding her plate up to eye level for my perusal. There in the middle of a lettuce leaf is the sweetest little baby (I presume) snail, all light green with tiny antennae on its head, wiggling away and a little green shell on its back and he (could be a she I guess) was gently sliding along looking quite pleased with itself. Looking at the lady I smile, she smiles back,

44

good, going to be a nice incident here, ' well at least it's an orphan, I hope!' I say. 'Maybe I should go and hunt for the parents or brothers and sisters'. At which she and her companion howled with laughter, which led to a discussion on how snails mate and how many offspring they may have, and where do they breed, do they have nests. I must admit I was sorely tempted to keep the little creature and see how it grew, but my over anxious chef took the salad from me in disgust and threw the poor little creature away, I still don't know if it definitely was a baby snail, or how they mate! Replaced their salad of course!

Another incident involves that life long friend of every diner, the human hair. I'm sure most of us at sometime have experienced the pleasure of a hair in our meal. Trouble is the little blighters are always on the run, no matter how tightly the band is around the ponytail or how closely the hat fits, or the scarf or even the hairnet on our Chefs' head, there is always one that escapes, may I add this is a rare event, not daily! I may also add that I believe a few customers may just bring their own in and gently albeit strategically place it on their plate.........oh me of little faith.

HEALTH & HYGIENE

Frankie - Health and Hygiene is a major daily exercise. Well so it seems, I am always seeing one of the staff come out of a corner with spray in hand, as soon as the customer is gone one of them is swooping onto the table and madly rubbing away. As for closing at night it's like gang warfare against germs. There are mops, buckets of hot water, sprays, cloths, polishes, brooms and that's before they think about preparing for changing the oil in the fryer!!

I've found myself a lovely little spot in Rosalind's office and now am making it into a very nice home. The reason I chose it is 1-she hates spiders so they are gone. 2-no one else really goes in there. 3- It does not attract other flies/bugs. 4-It's warm. 5-It is very big, well for my size. 6- I love snooping on her computer. Finally - Most importantly the Health and Hygiene people are not at all interested as it's away from the food.

Rosalind - One day in walks a pleasant enough woman, who smiles politely as she asks for the Manager, that's me. "Health & Hygiene inspection" she explains. Well as this is my first restaurant, and my first Health & Hygiene inspection I am somewhat apprehensive as to what to expect.

It's downstairs to change into her white overall and hat, question board out of her bag and we start. I am frantically trying to remember the temperatures of fridge's, freezers, fryers, how long to cool something, what temperature to heat food to, how long you keep it and so on. All of this carefully covered in my one-day course, a thousand years go, or so it seems. Which have now completely slipped my mind.....bother. The staff are looking worried, you really would have thought we had all broken the law and it was the police after us, not just a lady in a white coat. We passed. The next visit another lady another white coat, but this time to test the liquid that the ice cream scoop is dipped into, is it up to standard. Not quite sure what standard, as it is dipped into a container that has nothing but water which is supplied locally via. Thames Water, which I pay for and I guess most of the locals drink. A week or two later we got a nice letter saying all was up to standard... and here it is…

Dear Sir/Madam,

FOOD SAFETY ACT 1990
Reading PHLS Microbiological Sampling Survey of Ice Cream Scoop Water. R:. _Bistro, Peascod Street, Windsor._

I write with respect to the food sample collected from the above premises on the 14ᵗʰ August.

Following examination at the Public Health Laboratory in Reading, the sample was found to be satisfactory. However, please note that this result only relates to that particular food, at the time of sampling.

I hope that good food safety and hygiene practices will continue to be maintained at all times, in order to ensure the safety of foods.

Thank you for your co-operation in allowing us to carry out our routine sampling. Should you require further information, please do not hesitate to contact me on the above telephone number.

Yours sincerely

Environmental Health Officer (Food & Safety)

Now wasn't that nice of them. So we can all safely eat Ice Cream from the Bistro. This did not however increase sales of the product!!!!

- **WORKING WITHOUT WATER/ELECTRICITY** - When the lights go out and the water runs out, it's a real challenge to continue but you can.

FLOOD

Frankie - I must admit today started on a very funny note, Rosalind always arrives early and gets herself set up for the day, everything switched on, griddle, coffee machine, Panini grill etc. ready for the first customer. Usually a bit of paper work and a coffee and she is ready to face the first customer. She's still trying to beat every obstacle in her way. I will say she usually succeeds albeit a bit painfully sometimes. The one thing she hasn't learnt yet is not to rely on staff they, are always letting her down. Today is one of those days.

There she is in her high heels and skirt slipping and sliding in inches of water and she's no idea how it is escaping from what is called a 'dishwasher'. In front of her are all these smiling customers standing at the counter, who can not see below her waist, therefore not the floor and have got no idea what's going on, and the chef is nowhere in sight. I must admit I'm not keen on water although I've got wings they don't work to well when wet, so I am keeping well away. Three times she's gone back to the 'dishwasher' to check what's going on, there's water gushing from underneath it, and three times she's flooded the place, I'm busting a gut not to cry out with laughter, why doesn't she just turn the thing off...

Rosalind - Opening the Bistro in the morning is always a challenge, one never knows exactly what gremlins have visited during the night...lights that worked the previous night have suddenly given up the ghost. A fridge that was humming away perfectly when you closed at 6pm has died during the night. Even the till will take out some revenge on you and freeze in the middle of the first sale. Eventually I resolved every one of these challenges, sometimes by design sometimes by fluke. But one of the worst gremlins I met was on my day to attempt to 'salt' the dishwasher, we have really hard water here and every machine associated with water has a 'water softener' attached to it, and this needs salting every so often. As I have promised my self to do every job in the business this is my trial for today.

I won't bore you with the physical facts, but it does require a certain amount of bending and in my case eventually being on my knees, and my head inside the machine! After three attempts I am still flooding the whole place, and have not a clue as to why, Katrina gave me all the instructions and I am sure I have followed them to the final full stop. Would I dare not to? Anyway I carry on regardless. To add to my problems my darling Chef does not turn up, it's a lovely day and there are customers waiting for breakfast. I am alone, still new into the business and have not a clue between a latte, mocha chino or let alone how to achieve froth on a Cappuccino!!! Then of course we have the best breakfasts in town, one being the Full Monte, which includes everything, you could wish for, all at £5.95 with drinks! So we do get a rather good breakfast trade, and I am standing here with water swirling round my feet as I take on the challenge of the customer.

'Full English, Latte, Vegetarian and Cappuccino' is the first order from my pleasant happy smiling good-looking young customer. I blink take a deep breath (got to do this rather well during the years) and respond with 'Bacon Sandwich, filter coffee and orange juice only, with arms wide open and 'I am alone' then smile..."but" comes the reply, no buts that is it, think Fawlty Towers is my response and also point to the swirling water at my feet. With a smile he orders as I suggested, as do the next ten customers!!!!

I later discover I had not put the screw top back on the 'salt hole' in the dishwasher hence it just kept throwing out the water...oops, still lots to learn. Especially how to make the damn coffees, cook every breakfast on the menu and clean the floor at the same time!

NO WATER

Frankie - Oh not another water incident, what can I say she really has to learn how to handle these machines...hee....hee

Mind you it's a bit different today, we actually run out of water. It's the funniest sight to see all these grown people, waiters, and waitresses with any container they can get their hands on to move water. It starts off slowly and gets to a crescendo of laughing and almost crying as they all try to get the most water from over the road back to the Bistro. Rosalind has gone over to Millets the nearest and only open shop at this time on a Sunday to rob them of their water. Customers are giving their input, passer bys are adding support, or something of that nature and Rosalind is trying her utmost to stay professional and make sure the customers are still being fed and watered, well not on the

49

their feet that is!!

Rosalind - Well the challenge of the decade. Last night the water softener machine attached to the main supply had gone berserk, its 6pm and I was closing and whilst checking everything is off notice the kitchen floor is somewhat wet, well two inches under water actually. Paddling through the pond I find the mentioned softener machine has gone into its cycle but has not stopped and water is being pumped continuously out of the wretched thing. I am not exactly experienced with this type of device and basically pull out every plug I can find, as its run by electric. But still water, so I kneel in the damned stuff and find a valve on the pipe this joins the machine to the water supply and turn that off. Superb it stops. So clean up, lock up, and go home.

Today is Sunday, and we open at 9:30 am, so I get a lie in, but having had dreams all night about a flooded Bistro I am up quite early and in by 8:30 am. My nightmare of flooded basement has not materialised and I can breathe. Relaxed, I switch on all the electrics, fryer and coffee machine and peruse the papers. I like Sundays they are the best day of the week, customers are nice, no one in a rush and staff are relaxed, and we have music.

There is a very strange noise. I locate it at the dishwasher, which is not filling up with water, like it should be doing. I then fill up the coffee pot ready for a new filter, the water stops at half full. Ah... I need to reset the valve from last night. I do so and all is well, for five minutes. Then the water starts gushing out from the softener machine again. I hang the pipe into a bucket, which is filled in two minutes, staff are arriving and I am skidding around the kitchen, 'buckets' I scream, well the nearest we've got are mayonnaise containers, which are five litres, we fill three in as many minutes. I get to the valve again and switch it off. It snaps. Oh joy, well I can live without the machine. So we open. All is fine for twenty minutes until the coffee machine, which is a huge cappuccino/espresso maker just blows hot air, the taps all dry up, and the dishwasher is dry. No water.

Operating a Bistro without water is nigh on impossible, so with great thought I run over to Millets and ask for help, i.e. water. There are now five of us in between serving the customer trailing over the road with mayonnaise containers, and anything else that will hold water. Much to the amusement of the customers sitting outside the Bistro, who pass general advice on how we should carry them without spilling, we didn't exactly wash their feet, just

50

splashed them!

What relies on water to operate the Bistro, the dishwasher, the coffee machine, the ice machine, the toilets, the taps to wash salad etc. water to cook pasta etc. taps to wash your hands, the filter coffee machine, the coke machine etc. etc. By half past ten we had piles of dirty dishes, no flushing toilets and very frustrated staff, who were still smiling at the customer.

By one o'clock we had water, my weekend girl's brother is a plumber and he gets to us. A quick by-pass of the water softener via a new hose and it's all over, and the machine is left to machine graveyard. The staff stay, after threatening a walk out and the music is playing and the sun comes out, we are smiling, not paddling.

- **COUNCIL - Rules, regulations…and costs.**

Frankie - Oh dear I can just smell trouble brewing here. Rosalind is looking decidedly stressed and more than a little thoughtful today. She's been a bit down of late and I think from telephone conversations I've overheard there could be some changes coming about. The place is heaving today, and as usual one staff member has gone astray, and to test it all it's nearly Christmas so it's all happiness and 'Merry Christmas' to and fro from customers and staff.

When Rosalind gets uptight I have noticed that even the staff are a bit cautious with her. She does tend to be a bit quick tempered and not very understanding on occasions. Today though she does look a bit sad, and I must admit that after the visit from our man in beige I did follow her downstairs and watched her shed a tear, I think it's the frustration and a bit of the Christmas blues, its tough being alone at this time of year, I should know, well at least she only closes two days…. I might just pop over to her house for a visit.

Rosalind - With a busy lunch hour running and one staff down I am feeling a little stressed, and currently having doubts as to the future of the Bistro. To enhance this mood I am called to the door by an official looking guy. Outside is an open top van, police and several others, a tall guy in a beige coat introduces himself with 'we have come to collect all this stuff outside, you don't have a licence'. Stuff being 'A' board, tables and chairs, not sure about the plants! Oh and to add to it all we have a nice crowd waiting at the bus stop that I have objected to, and it is five days before Christmas, very business friendly.

I object with the statement 'I sent you £200 cheque for the licence nearly two years ago, the 'A' board I can admit you did refuse. (The fact that there are 'A' boards all over the town is of course academic!). Apparently Peascod Street, or my end that is, is a conservation area. With buses screaming past and delivery lorries driving down it the wrong way, and variety of cars going through every ten minutes or so (the barrier is broken) I fail to see it personally. Still that was the excuse I was given for refusal of the 'A' board….

Mr. Beige coat rings the office to check and insists I don't have a licence, so I request why my cheque was not returned as it had been done for the 'A' board (a mere £50). He decides to believe me and informs me to take everything in, I plead for time, and my Bistro is now overflowing! In between this drama I am desperately trying to serve customers with a smile, and manage an ongoing row between drinks and the kitchen. Mr. Beige coat lets me be. Warning it must all go, the fact I have no storage space does little to help. He does give me his card and says to call if I can't reach the right people in the council, apparently he's from legal, as highways could not cope!! At this point I must admit I could have burst into tears and just closed the whole damn place down. I really had got to the end of my tether with it all. Instead I went downstairs and had a few tears, even there I couldn't get any peace with constant shouts from the kitchen and I swear even a fly was buzzing about.

Two days later I finally talk to a person at the council who insists I should know I don't have a licence as I would have some paper informing me so. How should I know this, all I do is fill in the forms, draw the required sketch outlining the seating plan, send it all off with £200 and wait to hear. I never did, I am informed I should know that I would receive a permit, my first restaurant I explain, so that's no excuse I'm informed. So where's my refusal letter, sorry can't find the copy. Why am I refused, its conservation area, what with all the buses etc (now I can not win this one), and the police and fire complained. Okay, so, when I was interviewed by the police for my licence, why, did they talk about not leaving drinks bottles etc. outside, don't know is the response. I'm not going to win, this is the council. Well you can talk to your local councillor, but there has never been a licence for tables and chairs outside, I just know this is going to be long and hard fight and feel absolutely it's the last straw.

I should explain, that the road curves where I am and I'm on the thinner side, I have a very plain building, it is listed so cannot do much, having painted the wood darker which looks nice. But, the chairs and tables are my living in the summer they also let everybody know we are there and open!

My other encounter with the beloved corporation of Windsor and Maidenhead County Council is requesting a fridge be removed. Now I pay just over £1,200 per month as council tax. I also have to pay for my rubbish to be removed and often sweep the path outside, as the street cleaners seem to be blind. I am also constantly being used as a bloody public toilet as the council can't be bothered to sign post the local loos. (Apparently they do not have the ones down the road from me on their map) shit.

Anyway I call the local council for help in removal of a fridge that no longer works, as mentioned above. "We do not collect anything from businesses" I am informed. "Except my tax " I relay to Mr. Jobsworth. We only act as agents for the government who we send it to and they re-distribute it where they think fit, is the response. Now I am not a lover of our current government and in particular Mr. Blair, so I put the phone down before the explicates came out. By the way they will collect from you if you are private, so I guess I could wheel it home!

GETTING THE TABLE LICENCE

Now in Windsor, and probably the rest of the UK you have to have a licence for every thing that is external to your business. When I say external I mean blinds, awnings, lights, hanging signs, A-boards, and of course tables and chairs. This is an excruciating extended exercise involving money, paper and lots of time.

You have to apply months in advance so that the council can interview and place statements of requirements in the press etc. send out various forms and questionnaires for people to put in their objections. You are also charged for this, was £200 who knows what the next price will be when you read this. You are then charged for marketing, to whom I have no idea. You have to measure the width of the pavements, distance from road, (that's the Bistro wall not the pavement). Furthermore there is the measuring of the gap before you touch the nearest obstacle, i.e. from the bus stop, bin etc. You must also state exactly what type of chair and table, how many you require, size, colour. Also required are drawings showing where the items will be situated, and outline of the Bistro frontage so it can all be seen in the plan. Now I do wonder who the hell comes and checks all my measurements, I could say I have a hundred foot frontage, get the licence for 10 tables and tally ho! Anyway, they are the ones who decide how many you can have. I got permission for two, so I put out four!!!

RATES REBATE

There is no better joy than getting money back from the council, especially when you've paid out and got nothing in return, i.e. my various cheques to apply for licences for the tables etc. to be constantly refused, but the cheque always cashed. In my first week at the Bistro I signed a piece of paper that said I could win back some rates if the company representing me were

54

successful, then I would get a rebate, which would be back dated and they would receive 20% as payment, no rebate no charge. Seemed okay to me. To tell you the truth I forgot all about it. But about a year later I got a visit from these people who did a full overview of the property and measured everything, including the size of the air conditioning units. You would not believe what is included in the pricing of your rates, (business this is). You get charged according to the size of everything, the more space at the front of the Bistro i.e. selling area, the higher the rateable value per square foot. Even I can not bluff this and make the area smaller. Anyway this guy went off quite merry and feeling sure he would win my case, I must admit I was not even aware it was all going on! Anyway to my delight I received over £5,000 rates rebate, and some of it was for the year I wasn't even there. Which, gave me double the pleasure, after all the hassle Paul (the previous owner had given me) a great delight at winning something back from the bloody council!!!

- **WHERE DO ALL THE COSTS COME FROM** - from coffee to rubbish bags + VAT?

VAT *(value added trap!)*

Frankie - Admin, admin, admin. Its end of the month and Rosalind has her administration head on. As usual she is sitting at table 15, Panini in one hand and tapping away at the calculator with the other. Each month she goes through this ritual of checking all the monthly statements against the invoices, and each month she ends up on the phone to one supplier or another. Usually its Brakes, they never ever send the credit notes she is due, it took her six weeks to get back £20!

Today though it's different, the VAT is due and Rosalind has a real problem writing out that cheque, especially as she's learnt that in France they pay a lower rate of tax in the Restaurant trade, and our country has decided not to follow suit....can I hear the sound of zee French accent and countryside becoming attractive. Ermm, heard they have some very nice French Fly Mademoiselles over there.

Rosalind - Now I know there are rules in the VAT (*Value Added Trap*), as I call it, but no one tells you. So I decided to do the good thing and register. Trouble is in catering most of what I buy is VAT free, so I am always paying out, which is difficult to pass on to the customer as here in the UK we include VAT in our prices. Annoyingly I have recently read that in France the rate is lower for the Restaurant business, apparently this country have decided not to follow suit, another 'prevention of small businesses growth' from the government. Always fancied life abroad, perhaps the French accent could be inviting.

So I decide to call the VAT office, I have a long chat over the phone explaining its my first business and I just can not keep up to start with, could I have time to pay. Politely enquiring whether it was possible to pay little and often as this would help cash flow, I was informed that I collected money for the VAT office and therefore should be able to pay as they requested, no not in instalments, I had had my allowance for that, i.e. just one chance. In my first quarter I had requested a part payment, apparently that was my one and only time I was allowed that pleasure. Luckily I eat breakfast as I do all this paperwork and phone calls, it often saves me from saying the wrong thing. A mouthful of breakfast Panini can do a lot to stop the wrong comment coming out!

So with getting no further I reluctantly write out my VAT cheque and look at how to juggle paying the remaining statements and eek out my limited bank account.

RUBBISH

Frankie - Unlike my cousins and other relatives, I am not prone to hanging around garbage. In fact I find the whole rubbish dump thing totally appalling never could and never will understand the fly fascination for that type of hangout.

Well there is a bit of a problem, and the bluebottles are not helping the matter either, with their lethargic buzzing around the bins and then visiting the Bistro. I have had bit of a chat and they seem to be on their way out, there's a new kebab place opened and it seems the place is dumping some very interesting waste in their bins, luckily not in our road. I feel that the lovely fellahs will enjoy it much more and 'to treat it as a broadening of their horizons'. A couple of the chaps have scooted off down there so I am hoping they pass the good word and the others follow.

Meanwhile I'm following Rosalind out to the wheelie bins where the problem is, she is not happy and is happily talking to herself as she snaps a few pictures of the messy problem, could this be the next 'Tate Gallery' showpiece!!

Rosalind - Being a restaurant you create an awful lot of garbage. This has to be taken out to the large wheelie bins at the end of the service road. Now we are not the only people using this area, and it has been on several times a real bone of contention. People using the wrong bins, rubbish just dumped anywhere and everywhere, black bags being removed from the bins and emptied all over the place. Guess who gets the blame, yep us, because it's always the food that's found. Everyone may have forgotten the tramps I evacuated, perhaps they returned for their dinners!

Anyway it took some time to get sorted and I even went out with a camera and took photos of the rubbish being dumped in our bins. I should add that it costs me nearly a £100 per month to get the stuff removed. My rates don't cover this, apparently my £1,200+ per month for rates, goes straight to the government who then decide where to re-distribute it. Really did a lot for my belief in Tony Blair, not.

Another favourite with our merry rubbish collectors is the amazing attitude and customer service. I was informed by my staff that our bin was no longer in place, the bin being a huge green 5ft wide plastic container on wheels. It has a nice black lockable lid (one key fit's all), and I've plastered our name all across it.

Well upon this information I totter out to the rubbish area, this being a nice dark service road running around the back of the parade of shops we are part of. To add to the ambience it is under the adjoining car park. On this particular day I again have chosen a skirt outfit with the necessary high suede boots, cream. To look at the lids of these bins you walk along the concrete path which is six foot above ground level, but it enables you to see what name is on the bin, or at least lift the lid if it's open. The lid hanging halfway down the bin and takes two hands to lift, that's if its still attached to the hinges, otherwise its stoop down and look, great in short skirt and high heeled suede boots. Having wandered the whole gloomy place and lifted numerous lids, climbed over piles of rubbish, which includes mattresses, electrical goods and enough clothing to supply Oxfam for life, I am no nearer finding our bin. I should add that we don't have a bed shop close to us?

I call our happy supplier/collector of bins, and explain the walking of our bin, who informs me we are responsible, so I suggest to him if he is charging me for emptying it then he should have noted he was one down, and hence informed me, or is it that he couldn't inform me because he wasn't informed and they don't give a damn anyway. It was miraculously found a day later by my staff in its rightful place.

I should add that there are benefits to the taking of the rubbish out ritual, the finding of treasure…. My staff have come back with a selection of Barbie Dolls (all new), huge mirror in perfect condition found a home at the bottom of the stairs in the Bistro, new stereo, video player, old vinyl records, pots, pans, jewellery box, exercise machine, pictures, books, etc. etc. I could go on but I will run out of space. Oh and a golf club set with bag, unfortunately they were old and of no use to me. The newly active golfer!

I should mention all these items are not soiled, not covered in dirt, they are just placed near the rubbish area, there is a charity shop near us and it seems this is where items are placed for them.

Just for the fun of it I have worked out approximately of how many black sacks we used in a year, and the cost. Lets say we averaged 8 per day x 362 days (we do close 3 days), which equals 2,896. The cost of these being £2.99 per 50, which equals 47 pence per day!!!! Now add in the rest of the daily costs...see how many you can come up with...then see how many you incur at home also.

THE COST OF YOUR COFFEE.....

You may think that what you pay for a cup of coffee is somewhat expensive, well sometimes it is a little over-priced, but on the whole it is not. This is a list of what is involved to get a cup of coffee served to you at the table.

- There are the obvious basics, the table, chair, cup, saucer, teaspoon and the jug for hot milk. These are obviously in the set up costs, but have to be paid for.

- Then there is the coffee, milk and sugar and of course the water.

- More hardware needed though, the filter coffee machine, plus the large coffee machine for cappuccino etc., which also has to be, serviced regularly, another cost. Plus the dishwasher and the liquid for the washing up.

- Now you have the people, there is the girl who makes the coffee and then the person who serves you, two wages there. The pen and the pad to take the order!

- Let's not forget the overheads, rent, rates, water, electricity, gas, light bulbs, VAT and tax, plus various licence costs, including the one for outside tables and chairs.

- You have marketing, telephone, credit card costs, the till and the till rolls, the napkins that you know you are going to unravel from the cutlery, which then causes the cutlery to be washed!

59

- The table needs cleaning, this takes a cloth and a specific and expensive solution for this operation, and we do want hygiene, don't we?

- Of course then you are going to use the toilets, the toilet paper, the hand dryer. Walk up the stairs that have to be cleaned daily, as do the toilets and back through the Bistro that also has to be cleaned daily.

So perhaps next time you sit down and take your first sip of the black nectar, take a thought of all that was involved for your coffee to reach you at the table!

- **ROYALTY, WAR, MURDER & INFECTION - It takes more than this to destroy my business.**

FUNERAL

Frankie - It's a very sad day, the Queen Mum has died and today she is getting buried, the crowds are thick already and it's only early. I've had a bit of a shifty around the town and well it's hilarious, I have never seen so many bums in the air. Because of the interest in the Royal Family there seems to be an over zealous review of security. This being all our local police and soldiers reviewing the local drains. There are men in uniform everywhere, beautifully dressed in flak jackets and lots of ammunition hanging around their bodies. Oh I do love a uniform, must find out which way I swing!

Anyway I take a quick fly up to the top of the hill and buzz over the castle and view the crowd. I think she (the Queen Mother) would be very impressed, there are all nationalities officially represented and thousands of general public, all here to give their last farewells. Everyone is waiting to see the entourage of cars with visiting dignitaries to drive past. But most of all it is the finery of clothes that they, those general public have dressed in. Royal Ascot has not seen so many hats, but bless them all I have never been so proud of the English, here's to Her Majesty the Queen Mum, I do feel a bit of a tear coming.

After perusing the scene and hanging around overhead and seeing her Majesty off, I turn to buzz back to the Bistro. My God the crowd has moved as if one, and they are all heading down town towards the Bistro...Rosalind and her staff will never cope if even 1% stop...oh blimey this could be fun, well for me anyway.

Rosalind - I have driven in early today as I am informed by numerous posters and general mail shots that roads will be closed and entry to Windsor is going to be DIFFICULT. I guess no one who put up that notice ever tried to drive into Windsor at 7 am in the morning. With lines of men in uniform on horses, roads closed so our beloved police can put their noses down drain holes, this being whilst some other uniform holds their legs. There are uniforms everywhere, not that I am into that particular thrill. I do know there has to be security around our Royal Family but there is' little old me' just trying to get to work and I have so many obstacles that I feel by the time I have reached the

Bistro I've done ten times around the block! I do hope Her Majesty appreciates her locals going through all this for her safety, okay ours as well I guess. Seems to me there is so much money spent on trying to find the problem and not that much in defeating it. Me a cynic. Anyway today is the Queen Mothers funeral so I think I can afford the time for her.

It proved a quiet morning, lots of businesses have closed for a few hours as a mark of respect. I really was not sure what to do, but hopefully rely on the fact that she would understand my business decision to stay open and supply any mourners that may need a nourishing snack or drink. So far I've watched a constant trail of people going up the hill to the castle, not a lot stop, so I go for a bit of a stroll.

Within half an hour I get a frantic call the Bistro is mobbed. By the time I get there, I can hardly get in for the queues and the girls and guys are running everywhere. Within about five minutes I gather my senses and find myself fitting in with the swing of things, its manic! I should explain that we are the first real Bistro you find if you walk down from the castle, so hence our popularity with tourists and now the Queen Mother mourners.

I'll give them their due, they really did dress up, lovely hats, not all gloomy black and grey, I'm sure she was smiling down at the impressive array. For the next two hours we were non stop, I was truly proud of my staff. They really managed to smile at every customer, they managed every order, and regardless of how silly it was (some people do have a strange choice of filling for a sandwich). When asked ridiculous questions, this mainly from the tourist mourner, they answered without being too sarcastic. You can only take so many 'did the Queen Mother ever eat one of your Panini's'. All in all it was a pleasant day considering it was a funeral.

ROYALTY

Frankie - Well you never guess, we had Charles and Camilla in today, great laugh. It's the wedding later this week. I do manage to keep up with the news as there is always a paper or two hanging around. I have a quiet peruse of the headlines and if I'm lucky someone leaves it open so I can catch up on the gossip as well. Mind you I do like OK magazine for that bit, lovely pics in it as well.

Anyway back to the day's news, Charles and Camilla, well its 'look a likes' actually and there doing a practice run up at the Windsor Guildhall. The faces of our customers were perfect as they view the goings on. Funny thing was 'Camilla' came in all ordinary, then went upstairs to the toilets and changed...you could have heard a pin drop when she walked back in, then of course all the whispers started.' Charles' was already dressed so no need for a quick trip to the loos there then.

What a great story to tell the lads, the Bistro approved by Royalty...

Rosalind - Had the shock of my life today, came up from the office and the girls are all giggling and nudging each other, looking in the direction of their attention there are two very good look a likes of Charles and Camilla their wedding is this Saturday, glad they moved it to the 9th as its my birthday on the 8th April and I want a day off! They 'regally' order some sandwiches and coffees, regardless of that I still charged them. I believe it's only the Queen that does not carry cash!

It proved a great customer attraction for about an hour, I think word must have got out because we had a lot of passing trade call in for take-aways and 'I'll just have a coffee' sit downs. I guess you could say the Bistro became approved by Royalty.

MURDER & INFECTION

Frankie- There seems to be a very big dip in the usual tourist trade lately, its something to do with some poisoning or other. I can not quite pick up on the actual facts, but I know it's affecting business and Rosalind is looking at new ways of encouraging local customers to enter our doors.

I've had a chat to the pigeons, they get about more than me, and they say it's the same everywhere. This time the problem is something called SARS, we had the same problem when what is now known as 9/11 occurred. The awful day the towers in the US were blown up. I heard quite a few of my cousins were involved and have gone missing, its not only people that get hit in these atrocities, its us insects as well. I'm still trying to locate a couple of uncles to find out which cousins are still unaccounted for. I am looking to use Rosalind's computer here, think I've got the hang of something called the Internet. Luckily for me she leaves the thing on all day so I can buzz down to

63

the office and tread on the keys, I've taken a few lessons on how to do this I watch her from my corner in this office. Well she doesn't tread on the keys, just uses her fingers, though I think sometimes she is tempted to thump it, seems sometimes does not quite perform to her requirements. Nothing to do with her typing skills, of course.

Rosalind - Well we've had that awful day in 2002. When some nutcases hijacked planes and flew into the two towers in New York and now we've got SARS.

On that fateful day in September I was walking round Windsor with my lover Sean. I tend to grab some space during the day to switch off and it just so happens he was around. He had a call from his wife to tell him of the incident, we hurried to the nearest Dixons and watched the tragedy unfold. On that day Windsor died, it went deathly quiet and emptied, there are many Americans in and around the town, not to mention the hundreds of tourists. It was as if someone had suddenly switched off a tap, and let the plug out of the bath, because that was how the town seemed, suddenly drained of any activity, empty.

I walked back to the Bistro in a daze and told my staff, who had heard nothing of the disaster. You get very isolated working all day in the Bistro environment. That was the day I converted us from CD's to local Radio. At least we could then be kept up to date with what was happening in the outside world.

Overnight the business changed, it was amazing how many people were affected locally. Businesses that had customers in the States, our customers with friends and family there. One travel company eventually collapsed, this was due to the fact that they organised mainly business travel to and from the USA for an American company, because travel more or less stopped, so did they.

I had customers who were American suddenly decide to re-locate back to the States, being suddenly family conscious and want to return home, or their partners did. The knock on effect was truly like the ripples sent out after a stone is thrown into water. I heard stories of people affected by the attacks many, many months later after the event.

64

We got through the challenge as the Americans slowly disappeared. The coaches full of them coming to view the castle and wander around Windsor vanished, over night. We reviewed our menus and I reviewed our suppliers and the prices they were charging, it seemed it was not only my Bistro that was suffering everywhere had the same problem. No tourists love them or hate them they were the main stay of my business.

You cannot in any business prepare for such disasters and just how it can affect you, even though you are thousands of miles away from the actual destruction or event.

SARS did the same thing, again the tourist trade died, the Chinese who were a significant number amongst the visitors to Windsor just stopped coming. They were our pasta brigades, if a group of Chinese walked in, we would all look at each other and mutter 'pasta'. Americans were 'burgers'.

The Iraq war also took its toll on the economy and hence the tourist trade, again people became afraid of travel and spending. Windsor also is home of a couple of army barracks, so therefore I lost a few more regulars, this time to a war zone. One thing I learnt through these events, I was actually very lucky because I had a strong local customer base and believe you me did I appreciate every single one of them. Funnily enough I got to know them a lot better over the coming months and it was surprising what a variety of lives walked through my doors.

- **SURVIVING - Frankie & I are still going strong, and smiling!**

ATTACK.

Frankie - Well I've had good night, she closed early and I sort of pulled out the stops and gave myself an 'advanced driver' flying lesson. Lovely it was taking off from the tiles above the suspended ceiling and swooping through the cracks of the lower tiles. Zooming down to the floor and just breezing over the floor avoiding the table legs and climbing 100% vertically back to the ceiling.... ahhh. I must admit I did give my friend Walter from the Castle a quick extra sensory perception call to come over and score my performance. Nice to have someone watch you when you are going for gold, as they say. Afterwards after a few beers, kindly supplied by Bar 21, well they are just over the road, and I know Rosalind and her staff all go over there for one after work. I hang around for awhile, hoping to hear any gossip, got a little too close to Rosalind's' ear I think. She actually tried to swat me! I then decide to do another swirl, this time through the higher ceilings of Bar 21. Ugh so today I have a headache and not a pleasant one and there is a real weird situation going on below me. You see being a fly I have a good sense of awareness of not the nicest of situations, mainly driven by smell....

Rosalind - What a fun morning, staff are late, customers are restless and I'm the only one on the floor. It is also a night after a few drinks with the guys at Bar 21, just over the road from the Bistro. A bloody fly buzzing near my ear all evening has given me a real headache.

Now I have an old guy with walking stick enter the Bistro, sits and orders the Full Monte, well it is the best breakfast/value in town. Just makes me a bit nervous (I have lost my sense of smell during this year, another story). I serve the regular people, and with a turn of the head I have a walking stick at my head and the most 'hatred filled face' a breadth of space away from mine. Suggestion of smashing my face in comes out of his mouth, apparently I had not been nice to him. Well, I had taken his order quite quickly and moved on, is that such a crime? With stick raised and spit and venom coming out of his mouth. "He did not like my attitude, what was wrong with him? Stick your bloody breakfast," he ranted on whilst I stood there with my hand in the till trying to give change to a waiting customer, I was just a little concerned. What was worse, the poor customer who was trying to pay and get her change shook so much that she could not move from the spot, so heard all the insults, and

66

apparently took in the vile smell also. I stood my ground and completely ignored him, whilst also assuring the 'paying' customer that all was well and thanked her for her custom. I then slowly took her arm and guided her to the door, hoping I was not to hear the crack of my own skull, with the lady safely on her way and my head still intact I retreated back inside to be met with the intruder and roughly pushed aside as he passed on his way out. This dear demented man stood outside the Bistro at 8am in the morning shouting abuse for the following half- hour, not a lot of customers came through the door during that particular time.

999 TABLE

Frankie - There seems to be a joke going round that I really do not understand, it's all to do with numb, numb, numb. Now I do understand the fly in my soup joke, and we insects have a few human jokes....'what does a human get when they get a fly in their eye'? A fly's eye view of life!!!!!.........we like it anyway!

Just been introduced to a new one..... it goes like this...

A fly friend of mine was out with a group of fly friends at Bar 51, three guys and 2 girls. How did I know which was which, the boys landed on the empty beer cans the girls headed for the ladies!!!!!

Rosalind - All our tables are numbered, basically from 1 to 27, but there is no 13, but a 99, which is the tall table with stalls, and the 999 table against the bar. Well I should say that this is the numb, numb, numb table. This is from a joke (my IBM account manager told me in my previous life), which based around a woman having an intimate examination, who was offered some pain relief. My staff thought it quite hilarious, the punch line was' numb, numb, numb' with a certain action. So table 999 has become numb numb numb table! I don't think the customers have cottoned on yet

- **THE PERSONAL LIFE OF ROSALIND HOPEWELL** - More the past says hello, the present says goodbye and the future introduces itself, far too many emotions.

THE WIFE

Frankie - Everyone has met him, the lover that is. He came to the party Rosalind held here at the Bistro to celebrate the first year. Bit younger than her, she met him on one of her trips with IBM in her previous life with IT. (Now I do need to learn a bit more about that IT business). Am getting all the guys on e-mail, we all play on the computer keyboards when the bosses are not about and have taught ourselves a few things, and seen a few things! Anyway I dribble on, anyway Sean, (that's what he is called for the purpose of this story) has been here many times and they do seem to get on together, he even came over the day she had her darling Vermouth put down. So we all sort of know the situation, well that was until today…………..

Rosalind - its lunchtime and I'm cooking, the gay chef has again had a tantrum, which usually means an argument with the boyfriend, and it's a no show again, hence, my presence in the kitchen. I'm hot, frustrated and looking at orders for pasta, burgers, Panini and salads for about 15 people, who all want 'McDonalds service'. Happy is not a mood I'm in.

The Bistro has an open kitchen, so your face is on view to both the customer and staff, not always a perfect situation, still makes you feel part of the whole action!

"I'm looking for a Rosalind" a voice comes from across the counter. I look up and there stands a shorthaired blonde woman, a 'jewellery' ridden girl and an older man. "Yes" thinking its some mum who wants a Saturday job for her daughter. I already have one girl sitting at table 999 waiting for me to interview her.

"I'm Susan", blank look from me, "and?" still blank. "Sean's wife"….ooops. (I've changed the names, to protect them). I should at this point mention that her husband Sean is my ex-lover whom I had dropped three months prior to this situation. Well what goes around comes around. I am still cooking and smiling at customers whilst Susan goes into one, luckily the Bistro is busy and noise level high. I look as if I'm having a friendly chat, and inside

68

contemplating how the hell to contain this in a civil manner. Eventually I get her to agree to have a coffee and wait for fifteen minutes.

Anyway with now twelve minutes to go I have never worked so quickly to clear all outstanding orders and think what the hell am I to say. My staff are joking with me, the customers are smiling and meanwhile thanking me, and I am preparing for a slanging match, I think. Of course being female I am also conscious that I am sweating profusely, with hair flat to my head, dirty apron and flat shoes, so much for the image of the 'other woman'.

I actually achieve the impossible of getting no more orders and closing the kitchen for the required minutes, Why? Question the staff, because I am tired and need a break, I beseech them. I finally escape and throw the apron aside, hands through the hair and lipstick on. Passing the girl that's waiting for the interview, I explain its best she comes back the next day, and sorry for the inconvenience.

Taking a deep breath and telling the staff to manage, PLEASE, I request. I sit down with Susan. The jewellery girl and older man are sitting outside looking rather threatening, just adds to my fears of the slanging match.

Well her opening line shook me, 'your gorgeous, why do you need to go out with a married man'. I think I could have fallen through the floor, there I was sweaty, dirty and flat hair, how gracious is that of her. Her goal had been to find me, she had been round every restaurant and café in Windsor looking for a Rosalind, she wanted to see me and know what I looked like. I guess if the tables were turned so would I. She was furious with Sean and also annoyed with herself.

She talked of many things, all that he had told her, and how she'd planned to find me and the things she told Sean she was going to do to me, hence the jewellery girl and older man I guess. But, it was all very civil and I could have said many things to contradict what he had told her, but why did I need to, she had enough to mend in her life. I did not need to add to it.

I made a promise to her and myself that day that was the last married man I touch, they had suited my previous life style, but now I needed the support and care of someone who was mine, alone. Apart from this I respected this lady and my promise was made. We didn't' part friends but comfortable. I wished her well and hoped this was a new start for her and Sean, most of all for her.

Trouble though is, you can live with thinking is he having an affair, can you live with knowing?

Turning round to face the Bistro (had deliberately sat with my back to the main section so could not be distracted by the goings on), there is Zuzana with arms crossed and points towards the queue of orders waiting for me. "Oh blimey" I say, which is one of her favourite sayings. "Who was that, and why so long?" she laments. "I'll tell you over a glass of wine later…if you would help with the orders" a smile and she puts on her apron. Life goes on at the Bistro

NO DOG

Frankie - This is a sad day, as I see Rosalind come in very early and cry. After listening to her conversation with Zuzana later I understand and feel sad too. Her dog, Vermouth has had to be put to sleep. I met Vermouth once on the roof, Rosalind brought her in for the day, she let her have the run of the roof, its flat and surrounded by walls, so was quite safe and with a guard across the door every one who passed (on the way to the toilet, remember this is where I was dropped) gave her a smile or a stroke. Lovely little dog she was, big eyes and the blackest nose. Never tried to eat me once, even when I flew over her, she sat down wagged her tail and did a small bark, I swear it was a 'hello'. Bye, bye Vermouth from Frankie the Bistro Fly, I will watch over your owner for you, God bless.

Rosalind - If I could change a day, time situation it would be this day in February. I have had dogs for sixteen years, Silkies, which are a larger breed of Yorkshire Terrier with fur like silk to stroke. I'd lost one, Martini three years previously of a weak heart and various breathing problems, it broke my heart to have her put to sleep. Now her daughter Vermouth was going the same way.

She'd been back and forward to the vets for various things and still seemed to be enjoying life, albeit a bit slower, she was now fifteen plus years old. Both her back legs had been operated on during her younger years, she'd torn ligaments in both at one stage or another. She was the toughest little creature

70

and never a problem. She was spoilt and she knew it. A puppy face all her life, she was stroked wherever she went. She would take on the biggest dog if it sniffed her a little too long and stand her ground for all to see.

But life was not dealing good cards, she was having spasms that would cause her to fall down the stairs, or fall down anywhere. Her toilet sessions now took place in the kitchen at home and occurred at any time, and not nice.

This evening in February I heard a strange banging on the ceiling in the lounge, running upstairs I found Vermouth floundering like a fish out of water on the floor. I held her and she calmed. But this occurred again and again through the night, and she was just not there anymore. At 5am I called the vets, at 6am I had her put to sleep, she just wandered round and round the vets in a circle not knowing anything. The last thing she did was struggle as he put the needle in her leg, she hated people touching her legs. The smell of her in those last moments was awful as her body fluids emptied, from that day I lost my sense of smell, and still today it is rare I can smell anything but very strong odours, not good for a 'food' person.
It was a Saturday morning, I went home, numb I had so hoped she would go naturally. I went to the Bistro in a trance, crying for hours before we officially opened. I explained to the girls what had happened and then worked. I ordered from the Butchers, feeling like leaning on their counter and crying my heart out. I waited on smiling people feeling as though I would never smile again. I wanted to lock myself away and howl. How could people eat, drink and be merry.

I never wanted to go home, it just was not the same anymore, empty, no wagging tail, no pooh to clean up and no eager little dog to take up the park. No reason to get up half an hour early just for her, no reason to rush home to take her out. No little creature to sit with me at the pub and enjoy my dinner with. I was totally sad and felt alone. Whilst writing this it still makes me want to cry.

A NEW MAN

Frankie - It's a gorgeous Sunday morning, Rosalind loves Sundays, people and staff are all a bit more relaxed. Me I'm perfectly chilled had a lovely dinner with my lady from Cognito last night. I did myself proud, dressed up really well. Have met a fellow fly that lives over the tailors down the road. Gets loads of pieces of cloth and can really design some nice stuff. He's (that's Ben) been watching his tailor and learning the trade, so moi, one of the smarter chappies around Windsor has taken up his offer of being a model for his designs.

Anyway I rattle on, leave all that until later might write my own book I think. Let's get back to now, I have had a nice long shower, there is a dripping tap in the washrooms, and some lovely new soap so I smell gorgeous!

I am having a nice fly around outside, lots of customers today occupying the tables, sun shining, and particularly interesting threesome sitting nearest the door. Out of the door pops our darling Rosalind's head, 'hi, all okay out here' she asks smiling. I think one bloke actually dropped his fork. Here comes the breakfasts served by Eli. 'Who is that? asks the grey haired one to our Eli, "Oh the boss". He turns to his friends and claims to be in love…well he has never met this Lady before this should be interesting to watch, and listen to.

Rosalind - Another Sunday, I sort of love/ hate them. Love them because it's more of a casual day, hate them because I envy all these customers having their lazy Sunday breakfasts. Reading newspapers, lingering over their wonderful breakfasts, cooked by this wonderful Bistro, sometimes even me! Anyway sun shining I nose out of the door to check on our outside clientele. Note the group nearest the door not our usual type, looks more smoked salmon and scrambled egg type (yes it's on the menu, we are not all fry ups) than the 'Full Monte'. Two guys one woman, smile nicely and move back inside. Ellis comes inside half and hour latter and utters, 'you have a guy who has claimed undying love for you'. Apparently one of the scrambled egg guys! Yep just another normal Sunday………me thinks……?
Walking back from Waitrose, just another trip for that forgotten milk, bread, salad, etc. that we under ordered. Mind you can we ever order right, who knows what each day brings, and how many of the darling public walk through our doors.

72

Well back to the incident, there he stands looking at me. The 'undying love' type of guy. I have actually been out of any type of relationship for some time so somewhat enamoured by the attention. Which I must add is instant from him. Seeing my approach in his general direction, sexually carrying two laden carrier bags, halts me and begs me to join him on his boat later. After some discussion and laughter, I actually gave him my mobile number…urh am I being sane.

A few hours later I get a call from Chris, (undying love), he is on his boat and would I join him and his friends for a drink after work. Well me being me hums and haas, eer could you ring me later and see how I am getting on, could be a busy one today. (Looking at a near empty Bistro at 3pm…) Chris persists and another phone call an hour later, I give in. Anyway I like boats, and well he looked okay as well. Plus my staff and customers basically nagged me into going, I had put my private life on hold for too long according to all of them. Cannot say I had really noticed, if its not there do you miss it?

So by 6:30pm I was gingerly stepping onto a very nice powerboat moored not too far from Henley. I say gingerly because I went straight from work with my usual strappy high heel sandals, and this time with cropped off jeans, will I ever grow up!

So it started. This was to be an incredible journey that was torn between love and war, finally hatred. This book is more about the fun side of my life, so hence I shall go no further. It brings back to much pain and I wish to move on from that part of my life.

Frankie - Since that Sunday in June I can honestly say I have seen Rosalind swing from the greatest heights of happiness to the most depressed depths of loneliness. Even Sean did not do this to her. So it is with sadness that I note eventually she had to let go of this Chris, but unfortunately they got back together nine months later. Just to have her world torn apart. I think another story another book.

- **EXHIBITIONS & A CHILDS' CHAIR - A day by the sea, a new project for the future.**

EXHIBITIONS

Frankie - Rosalind has gone off for a couple of days, something about an exhibition. It seems conveniently this one is just down the road from her Sister's house. Oh and it's rather a pleasant time of year, Andrea, her sister, lives very near the sea. Our Rosalind does love water I have heard her on the phone many a time talk about the boat trips she takes with Chris. Well that's when they were perhaps talking, maybe seeing each other or she was reminiscing with a friend on both events. Well I've decided to stay here, going over the bridge and visit my mate in Eton. Been a bit of a long winter and I feel the need to stretch my wings and there is a nice new Eatery opened over the bridge, got a feeling Rosalind is getting ready to expand her horizons and perhaps I may need a new abode.

Rosalind - Being the owner of an eating establishment you get loads of invites to visit exhibitions where everyone from the Wine Merchant to the Sausage Provider has a stand. Some very exciting gold crested, linen feeling documents that come through the post and land on your doorstep have a delicious invite, such as wine tasting at the RAC club in London, others are little more basic, but probably more fun.

Anyway I took up a few, only one of the gold crested ones, these were a bit too 'up themselves'. Occasionally there is one exhibition that looks worthwhile. On this occasion it happens to be in Poole, very close to where my sister lives. It just so happens I can get an additional invite so here come the sisters. Andrea has now become my Purchasing Director, well you cannot be the owner and do all the jobs!!

Well its look out for the best food, try out every wine and OK look for new ideas. Well did we find one!? There it was sitting on a chair, no not a person a child's booster seat. All wood and metal, £50 plus for the glory of owning one, but it was saving space as it sat on a normal chair and turned it into a child's highchair, without the restrictions and moving a chair to make space for a Childs' highchair. Space is at a premium in a Restaurant so two were dutifully bought and transferred to Windsor. I must admit on exiting the exhibition we did have to sample various wines thus ensuring I was buying the best, well what we believed was the best. It's great when you disagree with the sales guys on the stand, because the lovely little lads just give you another glass of another wine to sample hic..hic..slurp.

Nice thing though this little show was at the BIC (Bournemouth International Centre) and only yards away from the beach, which also has a lovely little bar not far down the promenade. So we sort of strolled down to that drinking hole and relaxed, it had been a hard day.

BACK AT THE BISTRO - A Chair Project

Frankie - It seems Rosalind's short break has done her good, she actually looks relaxed! I must admit nothing really untoward happened here so she is not walking into anything too serious. Minor scuffles between two customers, a few too many beers here, Attila stepped in quite nicely and dealt with it. One Eton boy was sick, Zuzana dealt with that, one 'run away' no one dealt with that, too late they noticed the women had walked without paying the bill. Also the odd scream from the kitchen to the floor staff, the scathing replies back to the kitchen and finally a bottle of wine opened and a few beers enjoyed. Rosalind will never notice, me thinks not.

Rosalind - Here I am back at the Bistro after a couple of days escape. It feels like I've been away for an age. I've now learnt to switch off when away, and with the help of Andrea, some wine and good weather I managed it.

Place looks okay, the staff seem to be smiling. The takings etc. seem to add up, maybe a few beers light, and no doubt a wine or two. Oh well if it's only drinks, plus if I had been here I would have invited them all to have a drink… Zuzana bless her does inform me they relaxed and had a drink after work, offers me some money…they work hard let them have a few benefits…so I took £50 joking!

Well two child booster seats introduced to the Bistro and going down very well with the staff and customers alike. We have two awful cumbersome highchairs, so any reason not to drag them out is good.

A friend of mine, John, visits and I show him the new additions to the Bistro furniture. From this simple conversation a new idea for a new product is produced. Our own Bistro Children's Booster Chair.

We invested around £30k into this venture, had consultants and designers put our ideas from paper to finish. A beautiful 'plastic version' (well I called it plastic it was somewhat rather more sophisticated than that). Still over the ensuing months, years this darling prototype has been to Italy and back, via. Mamas & Papas interest. Reviewed by numerous manufactures and talked about in many a meeting between Me, John and consultants, opportunists and business organisations.

I have visited several manufacturers, walked around the factory floors and understand the size of the machinery 'tools' needed to 'injection mould' the chair parts. It was fascinating and I actually enjoyed the introduction into this world, but still could not find the right partner to invest into this venture, I have not given up, just taken a breather. To this date the Bistro children's seat is still sitting in my spare room. Whom ever reads this, please talk to me about this worldwide opportunity...............I have business plan, no money...well not enough.

Frankie - Well I think our tale is told, I am off to new places, a new abode and to tell of my new life in my own book. I have enjoyed this life with Rosalind and her staff, and those gorgeous Bistro Customers, but she has decided to move on and I will need to go. Really not keen on the new owner, looks like a real fly swatter.

Rosalind - I could probably write so much more, but I believe I have given an insight into the every day running of a Bistro. I hope you have smiled whilst reading this little book and perhaps had a few thoughts about your present life.

Next time you eat out, remember the staff have lives and feelings too! So treat them with respect and you will receive that extra added service, a smile and a more memorable lunch or dinner. Your enjoyment could depend on it..........

Writing this has been arduous, because you start out shining and everything is funny and in the front of your memory. But nearly 30,000 words later you kind of run out of steam. I still have loads more stories to share, perhaps a second book? But I believe now is the time to stop. I also hope to live another life through Frankie, my gorgeous ladybird/fly that has been my eyes and ears when I am not around. He is staying in Windsor.........another tale to tell.

Frankie – Me I am writing my own book.

Rosalind – Me I took a new path.

77

- THE FINAL CHAPTER - Kindly written by Zuzana Bowen
  A Bistro Saturday - a staffs view point!!

(This is written as Zuzana wrote it, remember my lady is from Slovakia, I've made a few corrections on basic spelling, but not on her way of writing, it would spoil the experience). Enjoy.

One crazy Saturday in The Bistro

Zuzana & Katarina liked to open on Saturday. While Katarina was sweeping the floor finding the odds 50pencies and 20pencies and cleaning the toilets, Zuzana made 10 Jacket Potatoes, baked few pastries, made some mixtures and cut some vegetable for home made soup so Attila does not moan angry that nothing is ready for the day. Between 8:30 and 11:00, till the next person turn up it could turn up in to a quite busy period but they could organize all the preparation for kitchen, bar and floor efficiently and did not have to share the tips with anybody else just between them. Katrina always walks to the Bistro as it is cheaper than train and Zuzana as usually got a lift from her husband Stephen, who takes the heavy tables and chairs out, popes for a newspapers, gets a latte, and sit for a an hour, while the girls prepared everything for Saturday. And believe or not it is quite a lot.
All the mixtures has to be ready, all salads has to be cut, drinks cooled in a fridge, deserts ready to serve, bottles filled up with sauces, cutlery wrapped, coffee blended, eggs hard boiled, cheese grated, oranges squashed, lemons sliced, boards updated and place has to be tidy and cleaned.
Boom! Grill is not hot yet and first customers - American family walks in." No rush, we have all day" that's nice to hear. We are no in rush...so far. As soon as they sat by the window and ordered 3 Full English and 3 milkshakes another couple of regulars walks in. They are seated down and passed the menu and the door is opening again, two more walk in with a baby. They are offered table in non-smoking area in the middle of a restaurant and Zuzana starts the welcoming conversation about how the children grow fast and how the grand parents are busy and unhelpful these days. Family is seated, baby chair is secured. Couple of regulars is ready to order. Two full English, two filter coffee. No problem. Order is taken, another 3 people sat down and start to read the menu. Let's put the sausages in a deep fryer to simmer (they go always first) and take an order. 3 youngsters walk in and another 5 Japan ice all requesting non-smoking table. No problem. Few more familiar faces, exactly 5 walk straightaway to table one. Couple with baby is ready to order.

Sausages are nearly ready, it is time for a bacon & hash brown to take their place on a grill and American style milkshake started flatting on a tray ready to go. Katarina takes care of 6 over easy eggs and runs back to finish her two cappuccinos.
"5 tap waters and one tea, after that 3 teas and two milkshakes, one chocolate made of semi skimmed and one strawberry from skimmed milk. And two full English and one full Monty instead OJ, apple juice and heat the baby bottle for about 20 seconds."

Youngsters want to order. Eggs for the couple need to be turned over, baked beans placed in to microwave, mushrooms goes in to fryer at last and bread in to a toaster. Another couple walks in asks for table for 4, two more are joining them in a minute. First breakfasts are ready. Shit, we forgot the tomatoes, lets pretend it is not healthy. Well, what is healthy in full English breakfasts?
3 lattes to go, one decaf, one dry, one week, decaf 3 sugars, dry 1 sugar the week one no sugar. Sorry decaf 4 sugars.

An old couple enters the door. "Just for a coffee, is that OK?"
"Absolutely, just take a sit, I will be there in a minute."
"So many coffees! We don't know what to choose!"
"And that is not all. Multiply it all by 5."
"Why is that?"
"Simply all this coffees can by specially made for our customers by Katarina - polish style,
Anita - Hungarian style
Zuzana - Slovak style
Chris - welsh style and
Abigail - English style.
Than, you can have a filter coffee in this styles as any other coffee."
"Oh, I see, so than can we have 1 late a la Zuzana and 1 late a la Anitta!?"
"I am afraid Anitta is not in today."
"Oh, I see, and is Zuzana in today?"
"Yes she is."
"In that case can we have one latte a la Zuzana and one late a la Anitta made by Zuzana?"
??? Sure lets make it unnecessarily complicated.
"That is possible."
"How much it will by?"
"That will by a la £3.60.

Group of 3 walks in, straight to the smoking table - regulars. Order no different from the one 6 months ago. 3 x celebration specials with double Bloody Marys. Anybody would guess - another good night out in Harpoon Luis. Problem, bloody Tabasco nowhere to be seen. Use chilli powder, that'll do it. Drinks are gone, nobody complains. Second sets of two full English are nearly ready. Before the drinks. Damn it! Lets quickly make the drinks.

"Do you do breakfasts," big bloke walks in on his own, " there is 7 of us outside."
"Sure come in and take a sit, left smoking, right no smoking."

The toasts are burning, lets' quickly make a new ones.
Three breakfast Panini, two with crispy bacon, one extra tomato.
Katarina breaks the eggs on the grill, lies down 3 rashers of bacon, opens tin with baked beans, places three portions in the microwave and inserts three slice of bread in the toaster. All in between frothing two lattes for an odd couple. One no chocolate sprinkle on the top.
The rush just started and we need to admit that at this moment we are really short of staff.

"Do you have a newspapers?"
"Where is the toilet?"
"What is the brown sauce made of?"
"How long before we served?"
"I don't have a cutlery!"
"In a minute, I will be there in a minute... Just a second, just give me a one second..."
Cappuccinos are ready to go. 4 more tables are ready to be served.
Two more popped in. Table for two?
Baby bottle nearly melted, Americans are ready to pay, no rush. 4 completed breakfasts are getting cold. Table two is seeking an attention.

Nooooo!

"Steve get your English arse of the chair, pass the newspapers on table 5 and take an order from table one...and make 5 tap waters...and sit these two guys on table 12."
"What two guys?" Stephen is closing sport page. "Which one is table 12? How to make a tap water?"

OK, calm down, Zuzana, this is how to make a tap water. "Take 5 clean glasses, put them next to each other under the tap, then press the button saying "TAP WATER" keep holding until the glass is nearly full and then do the same with the rest. Comprende?" This is how to explain to a welder how to make 5 tap waters at 10.30 on Saturday morning for 5 Japanese.
Bills for Americans. £2 tips.
"Have a nice day!"
"Thank you, you too!" Yes, we trying to.
3 celebrations specials ready to go. Table of four wants to order.
Odd couple also decided to have some breakfast. Table 3 still waiting for latte and a tea. Japanese are asking for ketchup.

"Are you working here?" that was to Stephen. "Occasionally." he answers carrying wobbly tray with 3 cappuccinos, one decaf coffee and earl gray tea to a wrong table. "There is no light in ladies."
"I am going to ladies, the light is off, do you have a spare bulbs?"
"Don't worry about the bulbs now and take the ketchup to Japanese and ask table 4 what they want…and open the back door to make a breeze."
"How do I ask it? "
"Just be polite and apologies for the long wait."
"What do you want mate?" welders style to be polite.
??? "One weak filter coffee with hot milk and one latte, with vanilla flavor, two full English, one no tomato, baked beans instead, the other with well done eggs, the one with beans extra toast and the other one with well done eggs plus mushrooms and no butter on toast. Do you have a mustard?" Steve has no pad to write the order down trusts his memory. On the way is stopped by two other tables for an extra toast and no hash brown changes and his memory fails.

"What do they want?"
"I don't know some coffee and two breakfast, I forgot, go and do it yourself!"
"Ok, ok, keep your hair on, come in and wash some cappuccino cups while Katarina is cooking, we are running low, I take the order."
Table 12 sorted. Sausages are simmering, bacon frying, mushrooms deep-frying, bb heating up in a microwave, toast toasting. So far everything is under the control.
Japanese are ready to pay. Individually of course, all with brand new crispy 50 pound note. Leave no tips. Japanese never leave tips. They are expressing their thanks by different way. By the interest in a country, and there we go, they are extremely thankful. Where is the castle, how to get there, what time it is open,

is the queen in is today, what is the weather like this time of year, is it going stop raining today? Of course it is going to stop raining. As far as I remember, ever since, up to now it always stopped...until it started again. Than they make a couple of pictures with Katharine 'The Chef' and the normal Saturday things and then they finally bugger off.
3 more full English, as it goes. Thanks God. And bill for table one. They have no change, we neither. "Fine, keep the rest." Absolutely.

10:30am Stephen capitulate and leaves the Bistro swearing never ever give a lift to Zuzana again, no matter how much he loves her. Dishwasher is already working overtime and more orders are coming through. Two mixed up tables, one cut finger, two broken glasses, one burnt hand, 2 completely messed up t-shirts and huge pile of washing. Only God knows himself, how many white t-shirts were christened by oil or ketchup's marks in this kitchen.

Welcome to the Bistro on Saturday morning!
One hour later:

OK, first load is done, £460 in a till, £12.63 in a tip box. Not bad?!
Attila walks in. In fact bicycles in and break hard in front of the till. "G' morning, girls!" Bicycle goes straight to a fire exit way. There is no point of explaining, that this is a fire exit. We leave it. Attila had evidently great night out with his roommates. His face still squashed from the pillow, irises suspiciously wide open, desperately longing for double espresso and roll ups. But the day only started.
Special boards need to go out.
"So, Attila, what is the special today?"
"Pigeon shits Panini with salad or fries...avocado, extra 80 pence."
"I am serious I need to write the boards."
"I don't know I did not make my mind yet. Do I look I made my mind yet?"
"Definitely not."
It is nearly 12 o' clock, Rosalind is going to kill us but Gregory also starts at 12 and it his birthday. No matter how much charming he is, he is a lazy shit. Chatting with the girls, drinking freshly squeezed orange juice, that's him. We need to inspirited by him, have to find a way to make him working. Anything. Taking the special board, Zuzana write on it with Hi-visual orange chalk: HAPPY BIRTHDAY, GREGORY! And puts it up to a Hi-visual place outside

of The Bistro.

12 o' clock, Rosalind walks in with 3 Cognito bags smile on her face. "All right, any mail for me?"

Gregory walks in. 7 minutes late. Not bad for Saturday. Looks naked. No wander another of his long night out parting in Liquid. Greasy hair creasy shirt but never-ending seducing smile, couple compliments to girls how sexy they look today and lets go behind the bar for some breakfast. Rosalind returns the smile and ignores the rest going through the invoices. There is no time for sweeties. It is a SATURDAY. And customers from table 5 want to pay. "Which one of you is Gregory?"

"Me..." Gregory does not hesitate to start lousy conversation with the old guy "...the most lovely and friendly boy here." The next is traditional, where do you come from, do you like it in here, lovely breakfast...bla bla bla.

Two pounds go in a tip box, fiver to Gregory: "Happy birthday, boy!" Unbelievable, he did not move a finger yet and has already five pounds from this old couple that Zuzana has fed with specially designed full English breakfasts and Katarina has blessed with her unique milky cappuccinos. Lucky bustard, this is exactly how it works in real life. women do the working, men do the talking. The special board is changed immediately. Gammon steak served with salad and chips. That did not make

Gregory to loose his shiny smile but finally he is on the floor. Chatting up the girls of course. It took Rosalind 3 seasons to figure out that he is completely useless for the business and stopped employing him any more. Well is not completely useless as his own designed association with David Beckham and adapted footballers image attracted couple of female teenagers. And really, the look and charm was there and everybody loved him, but hated to work with him.

Chris flip-flopped in. He is always wearing flip-flops. In case it gets too hot so he does not get too sweat. Well he never does. But one thing we have to admit, out of all of us he developed the best customer orientated attitude. Never looses his plot, or maybe he does, but he is a fantastic actor. Sometimes we wonder why he ends up here and not in a Hollywood film industry.

Lunchtime. All part timers are in. Couple boys asked for Abigail's' number. Rosalind is fuming that we waste too many napkins. If she ever knew, that half of them leaving bar with Abi's number she would kill us. Abigail is actually a good asset to a business. Innocent face, girlish smile quite few

83

customers stay for another coffee just hoping that she might come pick up the cups. Once she refused a date with regulars' son and they did not turn up for 4 weeks.

Restaurant is full. 8 people are waiting for take away. Rosalind is fighting two pedestrians requiring use the toilet. Chris seats down elderly couple and starts read the menu as they glasses were left home.

We are loosing one waiter, Zuzana is directed to the kitchen to help still recovering Attila from an independent night out. One player's off. Rosalind is on the floor wearing a high heel shoes. Amazingly she's managing well. Her friend walks in. Rosalind chats for ½ hour, another player's off. Gregory takes his first order, two bestseller Panini one tuna melt, all with salad and three coke floats.

Telephone rings.
"No thank you, we are not interested in new alarm system…no, thank you…no really…not even in a future… I believe you it is a good one, but we don't need…I appreciate your offer, but…no….no…no…" Sometimes you need to forget your good bringing up and hang up on a caller.

Portuguese family including boy of eight studies a menu. Father is counting all left change. Pound is high, but stomach is empty. 4x chips and one bottle off still to go. Order is ready. "£7.20 please." Disappointment, not enough change. Order is cancelled. Never mind, sandwiches from B&B will do it. They are sitting themselves at the breakfast bar and unloading their rucksack. " excuse me, but you can't eat your own sandwiches in here."
"Why?" surprise in Portuguese eyes.
There are a million reasons why, but try to explain it to Portuguese with English that goes as far as 'hello' and 'good by'. Chris is giving up. Orders are pilling. Dishwasher is failing. Table two returns their drinks. Coke is flat. Somebody has to change the gas. Katarina is exhausted. She swears, in polish of course. Attila wants more money. Chris keeps smiling, taking piss of customers in his own intellectual way, they do not realize. Chris is in his element, planning to earn couple glasses of wine on the end of his shift. After hard day Rosalind always offers. Zuzana and Chris never say NO.

American family is placing an order. "What is cheese & tomato sandwich?"
"That is a sandwich with cheese and tomato in it." Chris is giving a full

explanation.

"Aaghh, I see, and what is ham and cheese sandwich?"

"That is a sandwich with ham and cheese in it."

"Oh, that means, that cheese and onion sandwich is just a sandwich with just a cheese and onion in it, right?"

"That's correct," wow we are getting somewhere.

"And what is an American style milkshake?"

"That is an milkshake shaken to American taste."

"Fantastic!"

American positivism always amazes, fantastic, delicious, spectacular, and excellent. You can serve them a deep fried shit in a burger bun, they will think it is absolutely fabulous.

3 lads in checked shirts reluctantly stand by the door pushing the oldest one in the front.

"Table for 3?"

"Yes!"

"Come with me!" Zuzana grabs the menus and leads them to an empty table. The oldest one speaks with polish accent. "Can I speak to manager, I am looking for a job."

Blimme me, they must open a new job center behind the corner, this question was popped today at least 10 times. Attila's on a fag break he can deal with it, end of the day it is for him in the kitchen.

"What kind of job you looking for?"

"Kitchen, anything." says the guy.

"Yes, kitchen anything." repeats the small one behind him.

"Kitchen porter." said the third one with advanced vocabulary.

"Have you ever worked in the kitchen?"

"Yes."

"What did you do?"

"Yes, yes, no problem."

??? "So, can you cook?"

"Yes, kitchen, anything."

"Where did you work before?"

"Yes, no problem."

Ok, this is going by a tough one. "Look guys, this is not a very good time for an interview, come tomorrow and speak to Chris. OK?

"OK, kitchen, anything, no problem."

Lady about 70 or more walks in with upset face. She was here last night and had a wine and a dinner with her husband. Her husband did not feel well afterwards, in fact he was throwing out all night. Nothing unusual in their age, but the lady insisting on compensation as she blames a restaurant for the inconveniences. And demand to speak to a manager. Rosalind popped to Cognito, Chris is busy with Japan ice. Zuzana takes the responsibility. She was working yesterday, but does not recall the events taking the place.
"Where were you sitting?"
"By the window."
"By this window?" she points at the table 22 the only table by the window to put the details together.
"No, no that window, that was a small table."
"But this is the only table by the window as you can see yourself."
"I don't remember where about we were sitting, I am telling you my husband was sick all night, he is a diabetic and is in a very bad condition. And I am so distressed."
"OK, ok I am very sorry."
"He actually did not feel because of his arteries and could not walk properly that's why we sat by the window. He started feel rough after that first wine, he had to go to toilet, I am telling you the wine was old and corked." the lady was adamant.
"What time was this?" Zuzana starts the investigation.
"About 7, 7:30 pm, a boy served us."
"But we are not open till 7:30 we're closing at Six O'clock. Are you sure it was here?"

"Do not try to trick me, young lady, of course it was here, I remember the bar" she point at Attila's kitchen "young Chinese boy served us."
"I am afraid we do not employ a Chinese waiter here."
"Oh, maybe he was not Chinese just look like. Well I am terribly sorry but I am not leaving without a compensation, this is disgusting, absolutely disgusting."
"Please, don't get upset, this has to be put straight. So you are saying, that you were here about 7:30 sitting at the table by the window…"
"That's correct."
"…were served by Chinese boy and used the toilet upstairs!"
"No, no, young lady, listen to me, my husband suffers from arteries, he cannot walk up the stairs and down the stairs, and I am fed up of repeating myself."
"But our toilets are upstairs, we don't have any toilets downstairs." Something

is not right in this story.

"May I ask you madam what did you order?"

"You certainly can, it was some steak salad with artichokes and avocado with garlic mayonnaise, I am sure the mayonnaise was off, it did smell like it was refrigerated for weeks, some ciabatta and..."

"Sorry madam, I need to stop you, the dish you just described is not on our menu, we do not serve such a dish, are you absolutely sure it was here, in The Bistro?"

"Absolutely, listen to me young lady one more time, I did not come here to argue with you. My husband worked 40 years in Army and got a medal for his achievements. He is an honourable person. I am 73, I am a pensioner, and I brought up 6 children. My youngest son is an Environmental planning manager, married a welsh girl and have a three lovely little boys. I am not a liar. My oldest daughter Helen is a teacher in Reading, her son Jason...(Oh yes tell me about your family tree, I am all yours.)...lives in South Africa and grandson Michael studying in Bracknell...daughter in law is in accounting...cuisine will move a house next week...dog Zara had an injection on Friday... neigh borough had replaced hip two month ago and recovering well...And I am not leaving without my money having back and some sort of compensation as a gesture of good will for causing my husband bad stomach." Maybe even arteries.

??? Zuzana is flattered and capitulates. "Sure, sure, just give me your receipt and we can sort it here and now."

"Absolutely" lady shrugged in victory and opens old Mark s& Spencer black bag full of every day's life necessities from unwrapped sticky sweets to birth certificates of all her 6 children.

"There we go" she produces sticky, scrambled piece of paper.

"Aaaaa, this is the mystery!"

HSBS debit card, £43,95 paid to Claudio's, 34 Peascod Street. There is the explanation. It took Zuzana another 20 minutes to explain the mistake the lady made and another 5 minutes to walk her to Claudio's.

Finally she's gone, back to work.

Gregory just manages to get a date with a pretty 18 years old Asian girl - Jasmine. God help us. Telephone rings. Chris answers. "What, Rosalind, oh you did not know? She died couple of days ago, yeerh, car crash..." Phone is silent for a while, then..."Oh I see, OK, I call on Monday."

"Great idea, Good bye."

"How long before we are served, we are waiting for 20 minutes?"

87

Where is Gregory? Ahh, there he is, behind the bar drinking OJ, where else should he be?! "Gregory, get your arse on the floor, your tables are waiting to be served!"
"I was only explaining Abigail, how to make double decaffeinated dry latte, slightly frothed with vanilla flavour, not too hot."
"With OJ in your hands, sure, get yourself on the floor NOW, Abi will manage. And stay there until further notice."

"Chris is great, he is doing very well. Just sold 3 De-luxe burgers and bottle of Pinot Grigio the only problem is, he forgot to put it through the till. Rosalind's back. Fighting 3 girls with cheap handbags by the door begging a permission to use a toilet. "No, it is only for customers"
"But we are desperate!"
"No, girls, public toilets are across the road by the car park" Rosalind is persistent.

Table 6 is ready to pay. Where is Zuzana, another fag break. Well deserved, but in a wrong time. There is not such a thing like a right time for fag break on Saturday. But Zuzana always thinks, she deserves it. She thinks, she is the most important, reasonable and hardworking person in The Bistro. Moment, correction, she actually prices Katarina tiny bit more than herself. Everything has to be by the rules and that takes the fun away. Sometimes. And she gets angry, God she gets angry and unlike Chris she can't hide it. Rosalind blanks it and takes over.

German table carefully count and recount the cost. "Funf und funfzich, sichs und funfzich…" Exactly. All in silver and cooper. No tips. You don't need to be a brain surgeon to suss out they are East German.

"No more gammon" that is from Attila from the kitchen. Katarina is sent to butcher to get some more gammon, while Abi is struggling with hand washing as the dishwasher is completely screwed (Understand wrecked.) Jimmy - the fix it all - is cursed.

Telephone rings again and Rosalind walks out for another 20 minutes.

"No more lettuce, no more tomatoes" Attila is dangerously running out with a salad and mixtures. Katarina' already back, is happy to help if he changes the gas for her coke tap. Deal is done.

"No more ice cubes" that is from Abi "and come somebody help to do some cutlery!" That is Chris's call. He understands and takes a little break from face to face contact with customers.

Table 4 is paying by credit card. "Rosalind, get of the phone!" (Need line for credit card machine) They gratefully leaving £3.00 tip on card. That's Rosalind's, according to her running the credit card machine also cost her. Never mind, she compensates it time to time by some bonuses.

"Where is the scraper? It was here while ago!" Searching begins. The scraper is needed now. It is not in the sink, no in the dishwasher, no behind the fridge. It is only a couple of quid, but that one was a good one. Forever sharp, perfectly fitted in a hand. "Stop. Everything stops. We will not carry on until the scraper is found." Search continues and orders are pilling. The Scraper nowhere to be seen. Another reason to have a cigarette break. Attila walks out of the kitchen and disappears behind the fire exit where the black bags with rubbish are waiting to be disposed in a skip. Use your brain. These two bags smell from baked beans and contain bits and peaces from breakfast, at breakfast time the scraper was still in a kitchen. They are dismissed. These two black bags contain potato peelings, ends of cucumbers and peppers. These could be the ones. Attila puts Katarina's cleaning gloves on and starts going through it. Soggy bits of paninnis, with chewed up lettuce mixed up with egg mayonnaise, sweet corn, rests of sticky spaghetti and tomato sauce squashed olives and mashed tuna coffee rests and dead tea bags. 'Aaaa there he is, laying in the bed of greasy onion and bestseller mixture gently moist with mustard and hummus. Common boy, it is not time for hide and seek yet, it's only 3 o clock.'
Attila's back few more orders arrived in a meantime, now 9 all together and 3 takeaways.

Time to take a lunch breaks, but nobody is brave enough to ask for one. Zuzana's OK. When you helping in the kitchen you always get some nick-knack here and there. Finally, Rosalind sends Katarina actually forced her. It is understandable. It is difficult run all day, than take ½ hour break and restart again. You prefer to run breathlessly all day till the end, then go home and drop dead. There is a Sunday to recover. For some, Gregory replaces her behind the bar. That is a clever escape from messed up orders and forgotten drinks. Zuzana and Chris will sort it out.
Pressure on the floor is slowly releasing. 3 tables needs to be cleaned up and

one English family to be seated. Rosalind takes her turn.
"Can I help?"
"Table for four, please."

Fat family takes a seats and mum reads the menu slowly and loud enough to be heard in conference room in the castle. She is the one wearing the trousers, no doubt, she chooses, she knows what is the best for her children and husband. Dad did not even beeped.
"2 times children portion of spaghetti bolognaise and two cheeseburgers, for us. Honey is that all right?"
"Yes, yes."
"And four diet cokes. That is for a figure."
Typical English dining, humongous dishes of ¼ burger, topped up with full fat melted mature cheddar cheese in white bun swimming in a real mayonnaise. And low fat diet coke. After meals two ice creams for kids and two cappuccinos for parents.
"Do you have a skimmed milk?"
"Sorry only semi-skimmed." Did you ever see a cappuccino from skimmed milk, it is almost impossible to froth skimmed milk.
"Oh, forget the cappuccinos then and bring us a bill."
Bet they stop for kebab on the way home.

Remembering the day, when Attila refused to make 4 De-luxe burgers for a fat American family, reasoning with his bad conscious, that he killed them causing them heart diseases. Very caring. In a food industry you don't care. You do as requested and charge. That's all. Although our menu offers large choice of vegetarian dishes and various salads, bacon, sausages, burgers and chips are still doing the business. Simply they are irreplaceable. So shut up and cook.
Katarina's back behind the bar and Rosalind pops to Cognito.(She must keep that place alive with all her clothes she buys from them). In 10 minutes she's back. "Zuzana, do you mind if I shoe off at four?" "Not at all." she kind of expected it.

4 pm. Gregory is leaving first. Has to, he starts at 5 pm in La Tasca. First tip share. Everybody gets £8.73. Nobody complains. Abigail also takes her share and asks for tuna melt baguette take away. Hangover in not any better so she swapped with Katarina and calls mum for a lift. Chris is awaiting his glass of wine. Rosalind's already behind the bar looking for corkscrew. Eureka. She's

got it and offers to these that stayed glass of Chardonnay. She pours herself a large one and takes it with her to the breakfast bar with a long report from the till. Quick assumption, short check, takes £1000 in a pocket finishes her glass. Corrects a little imperfection on her make up, restyle her hair and picks up her hand back full of paperwork for later.

"Cheers guys, see you on Monday, if you have any problems give me a call." Chris is gone shortly after second glass.

What a mess and few more are trying to get in. "Just a second until I clean the table. There we go, what can I do for you."

"Two jacket potatoes with cottage cheese and smoked salmon. And sparkling water, make it two."

"Sure, no problem." Zuzana's battery is getting flat. Does this have and end? Does this ever finish? People are non-stop hungry, non-stop thirsty, they would non-stop munch something or forever sip hot tea.

5 O'clock. Eton boy's time. In a last few month they become a regulars. From the beginning it looks like they are hiding from somebody, but end of the day, they should not hide, they are boys like any others. First 4 boys turned up on time. Under the cover of course. Who would turn up in Eton School uniform with box of cigarettes in a café bar and ordered beer. They sat in the very back of the restaurant in a smoking end and Zuzana walks straight to them.

"Boys you know the rules, bear only for those over sixteen and al least one chips with it. "

"Deal" says the boys "make it two chips."

Another bunch walks in couple minutes later, all squashed together hiding the little one in between them. Another 5 Becks and two portions of chips.

"Can I see your ID's?" The little one fails. "Is that fifth beer for you?"

"No, no, that is for me, I am going to have two, he's got nothing."

Very shallow. From the Eton boys you would expect something more sophisticated. One day they are going to layers, politics, and maybe mathematical geniuses. Whatever. One would be almost sorry for them. Life perfectly planned by parents, directed by teachers and restricted by tutors.

If the insulated parents knew, where the pocket money goes and instead of playing polo or football, the boys are getting a real life in a town.

"Ok, and no throwing out all over the gents, as last time, clear?"

"No worries Zuzana, cheers."

They are getting too familiar, they better be watched.

Time to start to do some cash in bits, washing ups and cleaning ups, otherwise

we will stay till a midnight. Calculator is ready. Checks on one side, credit cards on the other side, petty cash in the middle.
...+...-...=...+...-...=...+...-...=
Bugger! £26.13 down. Lets start again.
Petty cash on one side, credit cards slip on the other side, cheques in the middle. Calculator is ready.
...+...-...=...+...-...=...+...-...=
Bugger! £13.64 up. Lets start again.
Super extra developed Aiwa calculator for £4.99 from Rymans made in Japan, country of all brains, and always gives you a different result. Must be a human factor.
9 more Becks for Eton boys. Attila fancies one himself. "Zuzana, can I have one?"
"Only if you change the oil today."
Deal. Changing the oil is one of the most disgusting, greasy, dirty and stinky procedures in a whole food industry. You have to switch the deep fryer of and let the oil to cool down. In a meantime clean water is heated up for removing the left grease. Than you have to drain all the old used oil with burned bits in it through a detachable pipe to drain in an old empty oil container using various sticks and long hand brushes to make sure, the tubes and pipes do not get blocked. Using cleaning gloves is an optional, but highly recommended. Shame, we have got only one pair left that has to be shared between Attila and Katarina. There is always a solution. Attila takes a right one Katrina continues with a left one. When the oil is all drained into a 40 liter container that will be taken away for recycling, drainage is locked and the deep fryer is filled up with hot water and washing liquid. Scrubbing, rubbing and brushing starts, leaving more greasy bits for dishwasher who really deserves a good rest for overnight. The dirty water is again drained into buckets and big pots and disposed outside. Wrong? Yes but we can't risk our sinks to be blocked. This procedure is repeated several times with clean water until all remains of detergents are removed. It is a good one-hour job. 45 minutes if you are speeding above the legal limit.

"That's it, no more recalculating." The calculator released three times the same numbers. £4.65 down. That's good enough. We are only human beings. And considering, that usual mistake maker - Gregory was part of us today, it is peacefully accepted. Total takings £1700 with the 18 Becks on table one, two cappuccinos on table 22 and one hummus special on 15 that have not been paid yet. Everybody's amazed. And last tip share. Attila ends up with £12.73,

Zuzana and Katarina £25.36. That sounds like a satisfaction after all. And that is not all yet. Time to take rubbish out to the skip.

The Bistro skip happened to be next to a skip of Charity shop opposite the bistro. This seems to be the best part of the day for Katarina and Attila. We always wondered why they like to do the rubbish together.
God Almighty! One would not believe what everything people could chuck out. Close, toys, kitchen things, sport equipment, furniture, electronically items...and all working. Charities cannot sell electronic items as they do not have a guarantee and insurance. People do not know, that unwanted Christmas presents, such as blenders, car hovers, and hair dryers and straightness that were generously donated to a third world can't be sold and are chucked out to the skip. Anyway can't imagine anybody from third world using hair straightened. The other day we have seen a van loading with a charity thrown outs. Attila furnished all his rented accommodation with radios, videos, HI-Fi', s and televisions, and Katarina renowned all books, pictures and toys. Yes. sealing by finding. Rosalind told us million times. But what the hell. Skip wasn't locked and the things were spread all over the place. That breaches all Health & Safety regulations, so in fact, we saved somebody from a tragic incident. Anyway Eastern European people hate wasting and this charity skip was a sad proof of enormously wasting lifestyle of English society.

Six O'clock. Star FM is changing tune in to an Asian star FM. Great, exactly what you want to listen after all day. Eton boys are leaving as last grateful for that little bit of privacy that table one in the corner of the restaurant offers. "See ya next week." That wasn't exactly a Queen's English.

6:05 pm "All in?" Stephen walks in with one heavy table in his arms.
"Yes all in, tables, chairs, flower pots and boards. And sweep the entrance a little bit."
"Any chance for coke?"
"Yes but after you clean all the tables, put menus on them and some cutlery."

6:25 pm - All done. We are done. Attila on his bike cycles through The Bistro. Katarina is offered a lift. She refuses. Has an evening cleaning job next door in travel agency. She is invincible. Whatever. Everything is switch off. Burglar alarm is switch on. Oops, we do not have a burglar alarm. As said previously on the phone to the agent, we do not need any. We do not need any security systems. We are safe. We have our own systems. And they work.

Good night The Bistro!

See you again tomorrow!

We all need a drink now.

T H E   E N D

Photo: Hepburnia Photography

About the Authors:

Rosalind Hopewell was in IT for 15 years, moving up from humble account manager to the heights of Directorship.

In her early years she worked in hotels and bars and that is the extent of her catering experience.

Rosalind took on the challenge of the Bistro as a route away from the world of IT. By managing the long hours and hard work with a smile every day, she enjoyed 5 happy years. Rosalind is now looking to set up a Bistro on a beach a long way from England, with a boat moored close by for the odd day trip. Hopefully Frankie may join her!

Frankie The Fly is Rosalind's imaginary ladybird/fly is the pure fun creature that she created to tell the story from another view. He is a 'gay' chappie and loves life to the full.
He is now looking to write his own book about life after the Bistro

Introducing Frankie's pal, ***Ben*** from the tailors. Learn more about him in Frankie's book.....

Fly sketches copyright© of Eleanor Ludgate.

Who gets there first, is it the sea or the sky
Which, agrees they are the leader, and where they meet
Is it at that meeting point, they become one
Just for that moment in time
The horizon is that perfect love
Where two become one
For an instant, before they have to move on.
And when they part who leaves first
Or do they compete.

As the sky and sea say goodbye
They know they will meet again, at the end of each day
They have challenges to meet and new horizons to seek
Conversations will never be far away
If the sky says goodbye first, the sea follows
Then there will always be a tomorrow.

Love reaches out and touches us all
It is just a question of do we have the will to follow
Tomorrow brings another horizon
Albeit another time and place
Love has no horizon just an ongoing sea of emotion
Which ebbs flows and meets horizons
Love never says goodbye just caresses the moment
A moment of meeting another greeting
With each new horizon.

The horizon is over and the sky and sea have moved on
The sky sees the universe the sea meets the land
Land is limiting the universe shows other horizons
Who smiles first, or sheds a tear when the horizon is gone
The sky looks at the land knowing there will never be another
The sea sees the sky moving on and wishes to hold on to the horizon
A tear falls from the sky, the earth becomes opulent
Another horizon, or just another moment.

The sky turns grey and angry
The sea rushes to the shore and weeps when it meets the land
The land is retreating
The sea is widening and the anger growing
The land is becoming less as the sea beats into it
The sky has nowhere to go, it already covers the earth
The sea knows it can change using the land
The horizon sighs knowing there will be another world but when.